ALSO BY MAUREEN GILMER

The Small-Budget Gardener

Palm Springs-Style Gardening

California Wildfire Landscaping

Water Works

Gaining Ground

GROWING VEGETABLES
in DROUGHT, DESERT & DRY TIMES

GROWING VEGETABLES
in DROUGHT, DESERT & DRY TIMES

The Complete Guide to Organic Gardening
without Wasting Water

MAUREEN GILMER

SASQUATCH BOOKS
SEATTLE

Printed in China

Published by Sasquatch Books
19 18 17 16 15   9 8 7 6 5 4 3 2 1

Editor: Hannah Elnan
Production editor: Emma Reh
Illustrations: Hannah Small
Design: Joyce Hwang
Copyeditor: Bill Thorness

Cover photographs:
Al Seib © 2008, Los Angeles Times, reprinted with permission (top), © Nichola Sarah | moment | carrots | Getty Images (bottom middle), © Stock photo | Token Photo | cabbage | istockphoto.com (bottom left), © Stock photo | dogayusufdokdok | tomatoes | istockphoto.com (bottom right), © Maureen Gilmer (back cover)
Interior photographs:
© Tnash7689 | Dreamstime.com - Planting Tomatoes By Hand (page iv), © Riderfoot | Dreamstime.com - Greenhouse garden with vegetables (page viii), © Arinahabich08 | Dreamstime.com - Vegetable Garden (page x), © Xbrchx | Dreamstime.com - Mediterranean Stone Village Garden Vegetables (page xvi), © Millaus | Dreamstime.com - Oasis In Desert (page 2), © Angelstorm | Dreamstime.com - Kitchen Garden (page 22), © Haraldmuc | Dreamstime.com - Thuja Fence (page 36), © Vallefrias | Dreamstime.com - Cucumber Crop (page 42), © Suljo | Dreamstime.com - Gardening (page 58), © Photosil | Dreamstime.com - Truck In Agricultural Garden With Drip Irrigation (page 74), © Ben185 | Dreamstime.com - White Butterfly Caterpillars (page 92), © Constantin Opris | Dreamstime.com - Vegetable seeds (page 110), © Witoldkr1 | Dreamstime.com - Growing Broad Bean (page 128), © Boonsom | Dreamstime.com - Decorated Ripe Vegetables Garden (page 140), © Nadki | Dreamstime.com - Broccoli Plant And Flower In Garden (page 156), © Franky242 | Dreamstime.com - Brussels Sprouts In Snow (page 157), © Snapcreativeeg | Dreamstime.com - Farming In The Desert (page 178), © Maureen Gilmer (all others)

Library of Congress Cataloging-in-Publication Data is available.

ISBN: 978-1-63217-023-1

Sasquatch Books
1904 Third Avenue, Suite 710
Seattle, WA 98101
(206) 467-4300
www.sasquatchbooks.com
custserv@sasquatchbooks.com

To the University of California Master Gardeners, in hopes that this book will help their efforts to educate, inspire, and encourage organic food gardening in an arid land

Contents

Introduction xi

PART I: CONDITIONS 1

1. Sites and Seasons   3
2. Climate Modification   23
3. Methods   43
4. Build Organic Soil   59
5. Water   75
6. Insects and Pests   93

PART II: PRACTICE 109

7. Selecting Desert-Hardy Vegetables   111
8. Seeds and Seedlings   129
9. Seasonal Crop Guide   141
10. Essentials and Problem Solvers   179

Resources 191
Glossary 198
Acknowledgments 203
Index 204

Introduction

When the going gets tough, the tough get going. They don't give up. They push the envelope. They don't take no for an answer. And they don't let anyone tell them that drought or water conservation should limit their ability to grow delicious, healthy, organic vegetables. This book is designed to enable you, the average backyard gardener, to overcome the challenges of growing with a minimal water supply. Anyone can do it; you just have to tweak your frame of mind from half empty to half full. These chapters detail just how easy it is when you're enabled by a host of innovative methods that can yield the fresh flavor of success every day of the year.

VEGETABLES: WHY THEY'RE DIFFERENT

It's important to know from the get-go, though, that vegetables aren't naturally drought-tolerant plants. They evolved over centuries in climates where rainfall and water supplies were ideal for agriculture. Unlike an ornamental landscape that can be replanted with naturally drought-resistant plants or those adapted to local conditions, vegetables are different. They're seasonal and short term. They need water to produce large succulent leaves and fruits. Therefore, it's important to accept this fact and remember it as you strive to grow more with less water.

FORGET WHAT YOU KNOW

Gardeners often learn their growing methods from parents, who in turn learned them from their own parents, and so on back in time. Those ancestors may have experienced a very different climate with more rainfall. Or perhaps they emigrated from regions with higher rainfall. Others may have learned their techniques where copious irrigation water was available. Today these water-driven growing techniques, such as rows flooded to saturation, are not the best choice for a dwindling supply. In fact, they are based on assumptions that are no longer in keeping with our environment and can lead to some of the greatest water waste.

A NEW NORMAL

To grow food without the guilt of using more water than you need to, it's important to open your mind to a new way of growing. This requires you to thoroughly rethink how you look at vegetable plants in your garden. You must learn to accept a new normal that changes the look and feel of the garden in many ways. The old expression "form follows function" is a slogan of the design community that has always reminded us that how we arrange things should directly link to how well they perform for us. Therefore, growing crops in rows because that's how they are easily irrigated with flood irrigation may no longer apply to our food gardens. Rather than seeing massive quantities of vegetables, we can get used to having fewer, more long-lived individuals that are therefore able to provide more fruits over time.

ANNUALS

The majority of vegetable crops are called "annuals," a term that is derived from the Latin root word *annus* or year. These plants complete their entire life cycle in the span of a single year or, more accurately, a single growing season. All are programmed to hurry up and produce seed before they die with frost in the fall, since this is the way their species survives. This drive to reproduce is a powerful force that lies within our annual vegetable crops.

Tomatoes are ephemerals, but due to varietal differences, their life span or time to harvest can be more variable. For example, common tomatoes, such as Early Girl, are ready to pick in 75 days while Beefsteak requires 95 days. Tomato varieties designated "determinate" produce their fruits all at once so the fruits can be harvested for canning or sauce. "Indeterminate" tomatoes produce fruits over a much longer period for fresh eating throughout the growing season.

Knowing this is key to growing tomatoes with minimal water. Otherwise you risk watering a determinate tomato long after it fruits in the mistaken belief it will make new buds, flowers, and fruits later in the season. Once you begin to look at tomatoes and other veggies as variable ephemerals, you'll discover far more efficient ways to obtain generous harvests with limited irrigation.

IT'S A SUMMER THING

Most vegetables are summer annuals in temperate climates. They begin life after the last frost of spring and die with the first frost of autumn. However, there are two groups of vegetables that have a slightly different life cycle depending on where you live, because northern coastal regions are cooler and high mountains have shorter growing seasons.

One group, known as the cool-season crops, are tolerant of light frost and prefer the more moderate temperatures of spring and fall. In many areas these crops are sown in late spring, then sown again at summer's end for a fall crop. This is another example of how gardeners waste water by trying to help cool-season veggies survive the rigors of hot summer days. Trying to sustain these plants at the wrong time not only takes a lot of water, but also won't work under the best of circumstances. Knowing their preferences means you won't waste a drop trying to force them at the wrong time.

Warm-season vegetables need warm soil to sprout, grow, and mature. In many regions there is a designated planting date for these crops, which averages around May 1. The United States Department of Agriculture has designated the average planting dates for most regions, which is when the soil is warm enough to germinate seed promptly. However, weather can be fickle in some years so it pays to be more attentive to the weather rather than relying strictly on a calendar date. Otherwise, you risk watering a newly sown crop only to have it fail due to colder-than-average night temperatures or a very hot early summer that stresses seedlings.

REALISTIC EXPECTATIONS

Vegetable gardening is a very personal thing that is directly linked to your lifestyle and family size. There are so many variations in both our expectations and the area we have designated for the garden.

On one hand, growing lettuce for fresh-picked salads with a few patio tomatoes will demand very little space. You can even do it in pots where there is no natural soil. Conversely, a big family garden to feed the kids and provide enough left over to do some canning will demand a much larger space and proportionally more water.

All too often expectations are not met because these space-water-yield relationships were not thought out in advance. Growing with minimal watering requires more forethought to plan the layout of the garden, provide space for each type of plant, and determine the best method of irrigation to use. Failure to do so results in a garden that asks for much water, delivers little food, and may not survive the season. When this happens, all the water applied to date has been wasted.

Growing food in drier climates is nothing new, but for many of us it's a very different path to cultivation. It is the method of the future, with the specter of climate change, increasing populations, and dwindling supply. The good news is that the age-old techniques of desert farming combined with new technology and global innovations can create a synergy that could transform home agriculture in America. So whether you must solve issues of drought or simply believe that conservation is a duty to the Earth that begins at home, I hope you'll find this book helpful. The future is bright and filled with organically grown slow food that asks far less from the environment in order to reach our table.

WHAT'S YOUR PROBLEM?

Your home-garden situation will fall into three different categories that dictate what you grow and how you grow it.

Desert: The inland West and greater southwestern states are true desert climates. Folks who live in this region experience perpetual drought where water conservation is crucial. Growing vegetables here is a real challenge, not only because of the cost and scarcity of water, but due to extreme heat and very low humidity. These are the most challenging conditions of all for cultivation of food crops, but desert agriculture in places such as Israel shows that it is possible and has yielded many of the best innovations for water-conservative gardening.

Drought: When the lack of rainfall stresses water storage and supply in any region, it is drought. History tells us drought can be short term or last for years. California is notorious for experiencing extreme drought, not just due to inadequate rainfall but also because of the strain on supply from extreme population growth over the last 60 years. Great droughts strike every few decades; the last one in the 1970s nearly destroyed the winter ski resorts due to lack of snow. The cumulative snowpack in western mountain ranges is a vital source of drinking water for many urban centers.

Dry: Water conservation has become a national issue, not just one afflicting certain regions. Yet our agricultural practices are based on an abundant supply of this resource. Those who wish to live a greener lifestyle by reducing their consumption of natural resources can use the techniques for desert and drought water conservation to make their use of potable water in the food garden far more efficient. Water conservation in the food garden demands a new way of thinking about this crucial resource and how we use it, indoors and out.

Part I

CONDITIONS

If everyone lived in an area with perfect soil, just the right summer temperatures, and light rain every few days, vegetable gardening would be a snap. Truth is, these conditions are not part of the environment in many parts of the United States, particularly those west of the Rocky Mountains. Historic droughts, difficult soils, and erratic weather make cultivating food a real challenge. The key to overcoming these conditions is to spend more time creating the garden in the first place, equipping it with the innovative techniques that help to mitigate environmental challenges of arid zones or of places where voluntary water conservation is the endgame. Failure to recognize the importance of these conditions is why gardens fail, but when you can meet the challenges head-on, you'll have fresh vegetables every year, whether it rains or not.

CHAPTER 1

Sites and Seasons

Whiskey is for drinking; water is for fighting over.
—MARK TWAIN

Anytime you grow plants under less-than-optimal conditions, it's the little things that count. You must plug in to the details of your home site and the way seasons influence plant growth there. That means learning about the many little things and a few big things that combine to determine how much water your plants need and when they need it. Think of it as a grouping of stars in the night sky that produces a recognizable constellation. Once you're up to speed with the details, the big picture of your drought-resistant vegetable garden will be revealed.

UNDERSTANDING YOUR LOCAL CLIMATE

All farmers are weather-watchers, but those in arid regions are doubly concerned with the relationship of the climate to the health of their crops. Those who are seeking to grow vegetables with minimal water will have to be extremely focused on the weather and environmental conditions because they directly influence how much moisture plants need each day. For example, in Southern California, hot, dry Santa Ana winds will draw moisture out of plant leaves far more quickly than moisture-laden coastal winds do. Such nuances of site and climate dictate how to adjust

When in acute need of moisture, the leaves of this tomato roll up their edges to reduce surface exposure to limit moisture loss.

irrigation accordingly throughout the growing season.

In the western states where the specter of drought is ever-present, and where the dry season is long and unbroken, it's more vital than ever to recognize your climate situation daily. It's extra important when growing more moisture-loving plants such as lettuce, because just a single failure to water properly or protect the plants at crucial times can quickly end the season.

DETAILS OF EACH LOCATION
High Desert

A surprising percentage of the land in western states is considered high desert. This includes the Great Basin that extends from the western slope of the Rocky Mountains to the eastern slope of the Sierra Nevadas. High desert also extends

High desert can experience significant low winter temperatures and snow for weeks, even months.

from Idaho to New Mexico. What characterizes this region is its very low rainfall, which averages about 7 inches annually in most areas. Elevation of these areas begins at about 2,000 feet and rises to meet the mountain zones. Such elevations mean that winters can be very cold and dry, a combination that requires special care to grow off-season vegetables. It's common to attach heated

greenhouses to the south side of a building for winter vegetables. Summer heat in the high desert also is problematic at lower elevations. In these areas the grow-

ing season begins in spring like other temperate zones, but as temperatures skyrocket in July and early August, vegetables often become dormant in the heat or even die from stress. When protected, the spring-grown tomatoes, for example, wait out the heat under shade structures, then are pruned back to stimulate a second growing season after temperatures decline in early fall. With the addition of row covers or other frost-protection devices, the plants may be encouraged to continue well into the winter months.

HYDROSTATIC PRESSURE

In plants, the condition of being fully hydrated, with cells and tissues filled to capacity with moisture. The term is akin to blood pressure in a human being. When a plant can't access adequate water, the tissues soften because the individual cells have lost moisture too. Loss of hydrostatic pressure leads to wilt and other problems.

MONSOON SEASON

During July and August, tropical storms that originate in the Gulf of Mexico travel northward into Arizona and New Mexico. This results in a monsoon season, where thunderheads accumulate as the day warms and then rain falls in the afternoon. Rainfall can be brief but heavy. These rain events can be mild or significant, with very little predictability as to where and how much rain falls. They may be short enough that no water penetrates the dry soils and most runs off in a flash flood. This is the reason the desert of Arizona supports the giant saguaro cactus and a wide range of desert plants that may not survive in the deserts of Southern California and parts of west Texas.

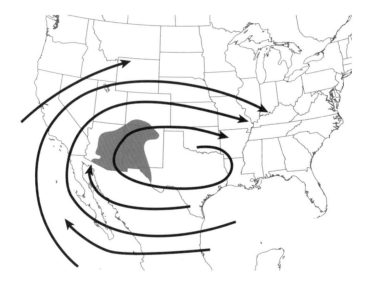

Monsoon season is highly beneficial to plants due to the increased ambient moisture it delivers to this region of otherwise very low humidity. While humid monsoon conditions are not as comfortable for people because sweat doesn't evaporate as readily as it does in dry heat, plants fare much better. The rates of desiccation are reduced at this time, and even if no rain falls, the plants need less soil moisture because they aren't compensating for moisture loss from the foliage. However, humidity can foster some fungal diseases that may only strike during monsoon season.

Low Desert

The most famous low desert in the West is California's Death Valley, where the highest summer temperature ever recorded was 134 degrees F. While this is the extreme, summer heat can average 120 degrees F in the shade for days or weeks on end. This valley is below sea level, which tells us that the lowest elevation deserts experience the greatest heat. In Palm Springs, California, a famous low-desert resort city east of Los Angeles, as well as in Tucson, Arizona, summer heat averages about 110 degrees F during dry conditions, while monsoon moisture can lower that number considerably. This extreme heat is the chief governing factor that limits vegetable cultivation in the summer months.

Low desert may have a near tropical climate where winter may be frost-free or contain just a few morning cold snaps.

The extreme summer is offset by an incredibly mild winter in the low desert. In some areas there is no frost or there are just a few nippy mornings around the winter solstice. These areas are at once the easiest to grow vegetables and the most difficult because the seasons are nothing short of counterintuitive. Experienced gardeners often retire here, only to learn their lifetime of knowledge simply doesn't apply. "Spring" planting is done in October. Then plants slow down for the winter solstice cold snap and short days, followed by a second planting time at the end of January. Crops then grow quickly as temperatures rise until the end of June, when the 100-degree days return. This incremental gardening year is not cast in stone either because the kind of plants you grow must be tailored to these mini-season conditions.

Mountains

Wildfires are such a huge problem in the western mountain ranges because these climates are decidedly arid. Most average about 16 inches of rain per year. Such aridity is proven by the preponderance of beetle-killed timbers, which are trees that became vulnerable due to lack of water. Trees in wetter mountain ranges in the east maintain good interior hydrostatic pressure, but in drought-ravaged western forests the trees suffer from low hydrostatic pressure. This softening of the growing tips allows beetles to enter trees here and tunnel through the branch to consume cambium, which kills the tree. Water supplies in many mountain communities are stressed by low rainfall and snowpack, making them much like high desert for cultivating vegetables. The difference is that the growing season in the mountains is much shorter and midsummer temperatures are much milder. Fortunately, mountains can experience afternoon thunderstorms that help crops, but this is unpredictable and, with very dry conditions, an occasional rain does little to change the overall need for irrigation.

Bark beetle larvae tunnel through the cambium layer of pine trees with low hydrostatic pressure, then exit through the bark after the tree dies.

Coast

The Pacific Coast can be divided into two different regions. The northern area, which extends from San Francisco to Seattle, experiences significant winter rainfall. The problem here occurs in the summers, which can be very dry for months on end. Though dry, the temperatures are moderate and fog can make heat-loving vegetables a challenge in some areas on the immediate coast. From San Francisco southward to the Mexican border, winter rain may be minimal and these cities are subject to much the same drought conditions as the rest of Southern California. The marine influence here keeps air humid so the desiccation rates are much lower. Only during the seasons when the offshore Santa Anas carry dry wind from the deserts do these coastal communities dry out completely.

Australian-native Leptospermum *has naturalized on this arid bluff.*

Gardeners here must be fully aware of how desiccation increases exponentially during the fall Santa Ana events in order to compensate through irrigation.

Inland Valleys

Some of the best vegetable gardening conditions occur in inland valleys. Protected from damaging winds of the Great Plains and deserts, inland valleys tend to be the best agricultural regions. The biggest problems here are drought, limited water supply, and rapid population growth, which put a strain on municipal systems. These regions are among the best for voluntary water conservation that goes a long way toward creating sustainable communities. In milder areas where frost comes late in the year, garden production can be maximized by cultivating a second season in autumn for root

Early missions built well-designed irrigation systems to cope with a long dry season.

and leaf crops. Strategies for extending the season and protecting crops using frost-control techniques such as row covers can make these the most productive areas for large family gardens, with enough yield for canning and preservation, but only if water use is maximized so that such practices do not stress community-wide availability.

ET CONSCIOUSNESS RAISING

You might not believe this, but understanding evapotranspiration (ET) has surprising parallels with spirituality. In fact, the two are quite similar because understanding ET requires us to wake up beyond our everyday reality to become aware of certain, often invisible or quite subtle, factors that influence how we feel. Everyone growing vegetables today should strive to increase their consciousness of the evapotranspiration rate with the same enthusiasm we pursue spirituality. The art of spiritual living is to become conscious of things we'd otherwise have

TRANSPIRATION

The process of water movement through a plant and its evaporation from aerial parts, such as from leaves, but also from stems and flowers.

EVAPOTRANSPIRATION (ET)

The sum of soil moisture evaporation and plant transpiration from soil to the atmosphere.

no clue existed. It's a sharpening of our sensitivity. It's the awareness of small influences. In gardening, it's a new normal that helps us see the world through our plants' eyes by increasing our ET consciousness.

Old-time farmers didn't have modern weather reports or forecasts to tell them what weather meant to their crops. They were hard-wired to these environmental subtleties and not-so-subtle cataclysms. These folks had a sensitivity of tiny changes in the light, air, temperature, and wind, as well as signs read from wildlife behavior that could predict the unpredictable. Today we are too often separated from nature at work and busy family life. Dependence on a smartphone has seduced us into thinking it's all about data. Truth is, you can't really get a feel for ET from a device. You have to unplug and start noticing nature, weather, and all the other things that help us work more efficiently with our plants. When every drop of water is precious, failing to do so means unmitigated waste both through our mistakes and the water loss that always follows inexperience.

ELEMENTS OF ET

The following issues are all linked to the ET rate, which translates into how much water your plants need that day or that time of day.

Wind

Wind is the chief factor in desiccation and increasing ET rates.

DIRECTION: Wind can be your primarily prevailing breeze or more violent, short-term wind events. Wind events will stress plants quickly, calling for more immediate measures to meet increased ET needs. Prevailing breezes create everyday ET increases that should be reflected in your standard irrigation regime.

SPEED: There is a direct correlation between ET rates and wind speed. Think of this like soil erosion. The faster runoff travels over soil, the more particles it picks up and carries away. So, too, fast-moving dry air passing over leaf surfaces causes moisture to be drawn out of the tissues at a higher rate.

TEMPERATURE: There is standard summer heat and then there are short-term spikes known as heat waves. When temperatures are hot and dry, ET skyrockets and plants will require additional water.

HUMIDITY: Some winds carry a lot more moisture, so these should be considered differently from dry winds. Typical examples are onshore coastal breezes and monsoon winds in the Southwest. While they can increase ET rates, they do so at a much lower rate than dry winds.

Rain

Rain during the growing season is relatively rare west of the Rockies, while most states to the east experience some summer moisture. Out west it typically occurs as isolated thunderstorms in summer, or as more pervasive monsoons in Arizona and New Mexico, and in the high mountains.

ABSENCE: In the eastern states, summer rain peaks in Florida with an average of 7 inches. Louisiana and South Carolina average about 5 inches. When summer rainfall is deficient in times like the recent drought in the upper Midwest that impacted the corn crops there, this has significant impact on home gardens.

DURATION: Not all rain events are the same. Summer rainfall often can be so brief it has little impact on living plants.

VOLUME: Summer rain can deliver a huge amount of water over a very short time. This is the reason flash flooding afflicts desert communities. Lighter rain over a longer period may only wet the soil surface and lack enough volume to penetrate the root zone.

ABSORPTION RATE: The type of soil you have can impact the rate that rainwater is absorbed, which directly relates to whether or not it helps plants. Dense clay soil has the lowest absorption rate while porous sandy ground experiences a very rapid absorption. Therefore a rain event can offer far more benefit to plants in porous soils than in clay.

CONDITIONS AFTERWARD: After summer rain, the conditions that follow have an impact on the rain's benefit to plants. When rain is followed by hot, dry weather, the soil moisture evaporation rate can be very high. Add wind to that equation and much of that rain will be gone long before roots can take it up.

Temperature

When you get hot, you sweat, and that means your body is gradually dehydrating until you can replenish your internal moisture. Plant transpiration is a process that loses moisture too, and temperature can drive this loss, particularly when there is extreme summer heat. Again, hot, dry weather is the most critical because this increases transpiration rates within a plant compared to high temperatures in humid air.

HEAT ISLAND

An urban condition that keeps city spaces hotter than normal at night. It's caused by the amount of heat absorbed by paving, walls, and structures during the course of a summer day. This absorbed heat can be significant. In open rural areas, the heat that accumulates during the day rises after sunset to allow cooler air to take its place. In a city, where there can be little to no air movement, the heat in these thermal masses is released into the surrounding spaces, preventing them from cooling off.

MORNING: When it's hot early in the morning, know the day that follows will experience maximized ET rates—increase water accordingly.

NOON: When the sun is at its high point, your plants will show their displeasure by wilting—try to add water immediately.

AFTERNOON: Plants in direct afternoon sun may wilt, but will rehydrate again once the sun drops lower in the sky, where the atmosphere close to the Earth decreases the amount of UV light reaching plant leaves—

(continued on page 21)

ET CONSCIOUSNESS GUIDE

WIND

Direction: What direction does the wind originate?

What it means: Know how close you are to the coast or other cooling influences as these directions of origin will be less stressful for plants. Wind coming from a drier inland direction increases ET rates significantly.

What to do: If your location experiences different wind directions, you must be prepared to protect plants from all of them. Be aware when wind direction changes, which can be subtle or very obvious but, either way, impacts the ET rates of your plant. National Oceanic and Atmospheric Administration (NOAA) reports often tell you when wind direction changes are expected in the near future so you'll be ready to adjust accordingly.

Season: Is the wind typical of gardening season or during the off-season?

What it means: Off-season winds have no impact on your garden.

What to do: When the garden is fallow, this wind will not cause problems except to structures such as fences, screens, and treillage.

Characteristic: Is the wind gusty between calm periods?

What it means: Wind gusts that are extreme can break or bend stalks of vertical plants such as sunflowers and corn. Maybe even blow them over, tearing roots out of the ground, which dries the tiny root hairs that are vital to absorption of soil moisture.

What to do: Be attentive to any taller plants in the garden that are vulnerable to gusty winds. In areas of blowing sand, be aware that high wind gusts can literally sandblast larger tender plant leaves unless they are wrapped in fabric for temporary protection.

Characteristic: Is the wind prevailing or gusty?

What it means: For plants to grow in perpetually windy areas, such as those where wind generators are common, there must be a windbreak or some other kind of protection, because they simply cannot replace moisture loss fast enough, even when sitting in a bucket of water.

What to do: Consider growing in a greenhouse or installing a windscreen on the windward side where the primary damage occurs. If persistent wind is seasonal, a removable fence or screen can be a visually pleasing option for the fallow time of year.

Characteristic: How fast is air moving—or what is the wind speed?

What it means: Faster wind draws out moisture more quickly, and it can cause rips and tears to stems and leaves called tattering, which allows excessive moisture loss through the open edges.

What to do: In high winds, so much moisture is lost from leaves that immediate soaking of the roots is essential to replacing such losses. For sustained high winds, increase watering frequency or drip irrigation to more times per day until the event passes.

Temperature: Does the wind feel hot or is temperature the same as ambient air?

What it means: Hot wind not only dehydrates the plant, it adds heat stress too, which is particularly damaging to cool-season crops. All kinds of plants with soft new growth will experience vulnerable tips that can dehydrate so quickly they wilt and get crispy in no time.

What to do: Protect plants with shade if possible. Saturate roots and water foliage to cool them down and reduce heat stress. Make sure mulch layers on soil surface are not blown away and thick enough to prevent surface soil moisture loss.

Temperature: Is the wind very cold and dry?

What it means: Cold winds can dehydrate foliage and soft growing tips in seasons when there's too little warmth to stimulate regrowth.

What to do: Plants benefit from being wrapped temporarily in row cover material that blocks wind but allows UV light to penetrate. Remember to remove it once conditions stabilize.

Humidity: Is the wind blowing humid air? Does water readily dry on your skin or not?

What it means: Humid wind may not affect ET rate much, but it can cause tattering and damage at higher velocities.

What to do: Use sheet plastic on a span of wire fence or another structure erected on the windward side to slow wind velocity while maintaining high UV levels. Wrap in insect-weight row cover material for protection to prevent damage and subsequent moisture loss.

RAIN

Absence: How long has it been since the last rain?

What it means: Every dry day after a rain causes a little bit more moisture to evaporate from deeper in the soil. Extended periods without rain can gradually dry out soil to the depth of the entire root zone.

What to do: If you turn off irrigation due to rain, it's essential to turn it on again promptly a few days after rain ceases so the depth of drying out won't reach sensitive feeder roots.

Expectation: In this season, what is the typical interval between rainfall events?

What it means: Knowing how often it rains in a particular season tells you how much moisture to expect so you can properly adjust your water application rates, dates, and frequency.

What to do: Adjust the frequency and duration of irrigation for the seasonal expectation, so it's timed properly when turned on again after surface soils dry out sufficiently.

Duration: How long did rain fall and how much rain fell?

What it means: This indicates the degree of soil saturation possible. A very short rain event may moisten only the top ½ inch of soil to offer little benefit to plants.

A drenching rain may penetrate much deeper. Soil type is also directly related to this assessment with sandy ground more easily wetted deeper down

What to do: Before you turn on the water, dig a little hole to see for yourself how deep the rainwater penetrated the soil. This is crucial in rains following periods of prolonged drought when soils are so dry it takes a great deal of water to rehydrate them enough to support vegetable plants.

Volume: How many inches of rainfall did you experience?

What it means: Weather services determine how much rain falls from a particular event by inches. If in doubt, verify with NOAA before making assumptions as often this can be deceiving.

What to do: Set up a rain gauge in your garden to get a true idea of how much water fell during a single rain event or the cumulation of a series of them. It's vital to check the gauge immediately after rain ceases to see an accurate level not influenced by rapid evaporation. Be attentive to dumping the rain gauge properly to ensure proper data.

Absorption rate: How well did your soil absorb the rain that fell on your garden?

What it means: Soil type can have a big impact on how much of the rainfall is able to reach your plant roots. Heavy clay absorbs water very slowly, so a heavy rainfall on clay over a short period can result in most of the water running off.

What to do: Familiarize yourself with your soil density and how long it takes a running hose to create a puddle. This shows you how fast or slow rain is absorbed in your garden. Some porous desert ground won't puddle at all under high water flow from the hose. There is a wide range of penetration rates between the extremes of clay and sand.

Conditions afterward: Is there standing water in your garden after a rain?

What it means: Standing water indicates a significant drainage problem. Roots of vegetable plants sit in saturated anaerobic soil conditions quickly lead to rot in the growing season. The problem is, symptoms such as wilt caused by rotting roots is identical to those of overly dry conditions, so often more water is added to alleviate the wilt caused by saturated conditions deeper down.

What to do: After heavy rain, take note of any standing water in the garden area as these will indicate where hidden underground saturation problems are likely to occur. Add compost to these zones to create pathways that speed drainage through the otherwise solid soil mass.

TEMPERATURE

Morning: Is your primary solar exposure in the morning hours?

What it means: Plants will tend to lean or turn toward the east and protection from afternoon exposure will reduce water requirements.

What to do: In the desert this exposure may benefit from shading structures from the end of May to September. Desert mornings can also be surprisingly hot during the spring so don't underestimate how much ET stress this creates on the approach to the summer solstice.

Noon: Is your garden impacted by structures that limit direct solar exposure to the midday hours?

What it means: This garden will experience its greatest solar exposure 30 days before and after the summer solstice which falls around June 21. It's also vulnerable to overheating at midday, so late morning water applications may prove beneficial to alleviating sudden midday stress.

What to do: Be aware of which edges of your garden will have the most shade in spring or fall thereby demanding less moisture due to impact of structural shadows.

Afternoon: Is your primary solar exposure in the later afternoon?

What it means: Afternoon temperatures are the highest and western exposure can be brutal on plants in the desert. Elsewhere this exposure may be normal but on hot days ET losses can be significantly higher.

What to do: Provide a shading shelter or vertical screen using 30 percent shade cloth to prevent burning plants during July and August.

Night: Is your garden within a densely populated urban area?

What it means: Be conscious of the heat-island effect on your plants that may suffer from radiant heat from adjacent buildings, walls, paving, etc.

What to do: Because heat-island effect is problematic after sundown, you may benefit from a short period of irrigation around midnight if your plants are showing wilt over the nighttime hours.

Change: Does any factor cause sudden temperature change where you live?

What it means: Desert climates can experience drastic differences between daytime and nighttime hours. These extremes can stress plants if not provided some protection just after or just before the start of periods when frost is expected—typically late fall.

What to do: Be prepared to use blankets or cloches to protect sensitive seedlings from extreme temperature change, which can lower their ability to resist dry periods or particularly hot morning sun.

HUMIDITY

Moist: In periods of high heat are your humidity levels high too?

What it means: The combination of high heat and high humidity is the optimal environment for many forms of vegetable plant diseases. Similar conditions occur in the monsoon season of the desert Southwest.

What to do: Be highly observant of plant behavior during these conditions because the earliest symptoms of diseases such as wilts and viruses look like the plant is wilting from dry roots when soil conditions just beneath the surface are very moist due to limited evaporation rates.

Low or no humidity: Do you experience the combination of high heat and little or no humidity?

What it means: This is the dual threat of the West, where the total absence of summer rainfall combines with soaring temperatures in July and August.

What to do: Heat stress combined with lack of water is the most trying conditions for any vegetable plant. It is often misunderstood in coastal gardens that are accustomed to the maritime climate. In periods of onshore winds or Santa Anas, these gardens suddenly lose this perennial humidity causing instant stress, which only vigilant gardeners can solve with prompt additional water applications.

add water if this is an abnormally hot day such as a heat wave, but be aware that some wilt is acceptable, provided plants perk up after sunset.

EVENING: In urban areas, heat absorbed by adjacent paving, walls, and buildings can radiate into garden areas after sunset. Without light, plants are not actively photosynthesizing, so transpiration rates are low.

NIGHT: Temperatures typically cool down after sunset. The exception to this is when the heat-island effect strikes gardens in urban areas. While plants don't need extra water at night because they are not photosynthesizing, water is still evaporating from the soil surface. To compensate for this, be sure watering is scheduled for very early morning to ensure enough is present in the root zone to stimulate vigorous growth in the cooler hours of the day.

NOAA EQUALS KNOWLEDGE

The one thing you can do with your smartphone, tablet, or computer is to plug into the latest in scientific weather reporting. The National Oceanic and Atmospheric Administration (NOAA.gov) provides the contemporary farmer's most reliable forecast. It's also the source of weather forecasting for TV news, so at NOAA you get it first and from the source. During the growing season it's wise to check your forecast every day to know the rise and fall of humidity levels, rainfall totals, satellite imaging, and other issues of concern to agriculture.

While it may appear easy to grow a vegetable garden, this chapter demonstrates how much is involved when we try to grow with little water. I live that way and have a real sixth sense about all of this. It takes time to raise consciousness, and in the process, you'll make mistakes. Don't beat yourself up about it. Just remember, you'll learn more from what you do wrong than what you do right. This is a discipline that requires us to reprogram our thinking to the new normal in food gardening.

CHAPTER 2

Climate Modification

*You know you live in Phoenix when the four seasons are
tolerable, hot, really hot, and are you freakin' kidding me?!*
—ANONYMOUS

Creating a vegetable garden that uses less water requires good design. When
growing in a less-than-ideal climate, your goal is to set things up to best meet
the needs of your plants on the most limited moisture diet you can manage. In
Chapter 1 you learned how important ET consciousness is to understanding how environmental factors influence the amount of water a plant needs. In this chapter we take it a step further by configuring the garden in the most efficient way, and show how to mitigate the negative influences that increase ET rates.

> **DESERTIFICATION**
>
> The process of fertile land transforming into desert due to inappropriate agriculture, deforestation, drought, or a combination of factors.

DESIGN MODEL: "PUEBLO" WAFFLES

For eons, human beings have been trying to grow plants with little water. The
Neolithic villager who carried the first water-filled animal skin to a gourd seedling knew agriculture wasn't easy. That intrinsic need to solve this problem over
the millennia gave us many models to learn from. Indigenous gardeners of the
desert Southwest, from the Anasazi to modern Zuni, learned much about growing their vegetables in a dry world. They offer one of the best examples of how

Desert gardens of the Zuni protect crops from winds with adobe walls and concentrate plants in waffle-like grids.

human beings can modify the climate using devices and techniques that directly influence vegetable plant sustainability.

If you look at a timeline of precipitation rates for the Southwest based on tree ring data, years of extreme drought appeared about 400 AD and again in 1600, with a lesser drought in 700. This shows that drought isn't new, but a factor of long-term weather variations. Indigenous tribes in this area practiced a unique form of desert agriculture, which exploited natural water sources and used them in a most efficient way. With no weather forecasting, their way of growing was unique and offers many learning opportunities for those cultivating vegetables today.

> *There is no such thing as a new idea.*
> —MARK TWAIN

Vintage photos show us the original gardens of the Pueblo tribes. It's easy to see why they were called "waffle gardens" because they are set up on a grid system using these distinctive parameters:

Perimeter

The outside boundary of the waffle garden is a low wall made of stone or adobe mud brick. Those familiar with desert conditions know that blowing sand and soil particles are quite common. These can pit leaves and tatter the edges, both creating breaks in the outer epidermis of the leaf to allow free moisture loss. These problems can devastate seedlings or immature plants, so the aboriginal gardeners realized that they could solve the

MITIGATE

To make something less severe, serious, or painful. In the landscape, the process of problem solving is often called mitigation of undesirable conditions.

problem by building a low wall. These partitions act as miniature windscreens to protect foliage from wind damage and reduce wind-driven desiccation, particularly in younger plants.

Interior

The interior low boundary helps to define individual crops or to group crops with similar needs. Some tribes were quite adept at channeling river or stream water or runoff during brief summer rain events. Channeling allowed them to force water into interior areas with great accuracy. In fact, contemporary aerial photography has revealed land patterns of massive channeling systems in the Southwest and Mexico, perhaps abandoned during one of the historic drought phases.

Straw bales make a quick and easy low wall to protect a small garden from blowing sand, similar to what the Zuni did with adobe.

Cells

Waffle gardens are composed of smaller cells that are identical to those of a breakfast waffle. Each small square holds a plant. The elevated edges allow water to be concentrated directly over the root zone. When water must be carried in a pot to irrigate individual plants, the labor and time involved demands that it be restricted to these crucial spots that support plant life. If you ever begin harvesting household wastewater for use in the garden, you will quickly get a very clear understanding of how efficiently this design uses this precious resource.

Double rows of squares, each containing one plant, concentrate water applied directly into the root zone.

LOCATING YOUR GARDEN

Some years ago, a marketing expert decided to create a vegetable garden in her backyard. This large, open lawn space was surrounded by lovely landscaping. She built a single enormous bed smack dab in the center of that space. It wasn't long before she realized that the bed had broken up the layout of the yard, making it the most dominant element out there. The remaining spaces were either too small or configured poorly for any future improvements. Then she realized that there was no water supply, so the hose was forever sprawling from the nearest faucet. Later on, she discovered vegetables didn't always look as prim and neat as they did in May, and there was little she could do to dress up the garden in the off-season. While this is largely an aesthetic example, it shows how people fail to realize that their vegetable garden is also a part of the landscape. In short, they don't think ahead, and the result is always inefficiency.

There can be no economy when there is no efficiency.
—ANONYMOUS

In many yards, there just isn't that much space. The smaller the yard, the fewer options you have as to vegetable garden placement. However, consider these universal location factors that influence efficiency:

VISIBILITY: Consider how visible the garden will be from living spaces.

WATER SUPPLY: Make sure your water source is close enough.

SOLAR OVEREXPOSURE: Beware of late afternoon sun in the desert.

SOLAR UNDEREXPOSURE: Know where the summer sun shines and where it doesn't.

DRAINAGE: Determine if subsoils exposed due to renovation will drain properly.

AGGRESSIVE PLANTS: Avoid invasive plant species or plan for them.

ACCESS: Consider if you can get a delivery truck close to the garden.

FENCING: Prevent wildlife from eating your veggies before you can.

Let's consider each of these factors in more depth.

Visibility

The truth is, vegetable gardens can be ugly during certain times of the year. If they're front-and-center like the example above, there's not much that can be done to improve the view. This is why vegetable gardens are traditionally set at the rear of a yard or off to the side where they aren't the primary element in the space.

MITIGATION: Install screen fences.

Water Supply

One of the most frequent causes of failed vegetable gardens is the lack of a convenient water supply. Dragging hoses gets old fast, and halfway through the season many people give up and let the garden die. Nobody wants to drag hoses, nor do they want to look at hoses running across the yard to the garden every single day. For the water-conservative garden, the location of a faucet should be your primary concern; it is crucial to installing a drip irrigation system that solves the hose-dragging problem. A battery-operated automatic timer frees you from the rigors and the potential waste of daily hand-watering.

MITIGATION: Learn ways to install or extend an existing water line (see Chapter 5).

Solar Overexposure

A garden is a lot like a passive solar home, with its long side facing south and the narrow ends aimed east and west. In the desert, the west side can be

Woven wattle screen fences allow air to move through, lessening the wind loads.

brutally hot in the afternoon causing undue stress to plants, so locations that are primarily eastern exposure with shade later in the day are more desirable.

MITIGATION: If you cannot relocate a west-side garden, then create shade cloth panels and structures to provide summer change.

Solar Underexposure

While shading can be helpful in very hot summer climates, it's desirable in other seasons as well. If shade that's ideal for summer is too great for a garden to thrive in other seasons, it will show it with weakened plants, increased pest problems, and poor harvest. In the desert, the need for shade must be considered in terms of the year-round growing season, not just the summer months.

MITIGATION: Thin tree canopies to maintain some shade while allowing sun to shine through.

Drainage

Locations on very dense ground will experience problems. The worst offenders are lots or entire subdivisions where the surface soil was removed for mass grading and the yard is composed of subsoils. These can be clay dense enough to make a pot, whitish limestone parent material, or a dozen other subsoils that contain little organic matter and minimal microbial populations. Above all, they just don't drain.

MITIGATION: Build raised beds.

Aggressive Plants

Certain plants such as willow, kudzu, or Bermuda grass can be problematic to vegetable gardens because they are so invasive both above and belowground. Where water is the guiding criteria, having these greedy water-lovers anywhere near your garden will lure their roots up into your carefully prepared space to compete with your crops for limited moisture.

MITIGATION: Remove the plant or shield the vegetable bed with underground root barriers.

Access

Most folks underestimate how much organic matter is needed to condition vegetable garden soil year after year. For water-conservative gardens, even more compost is needed for its ability to absorb and hold moisture longer than average soil. Smart gardeners often lay out their food gardens so they are readily accessible by vehicles. That way, a load of compost can be delivered directly to the garden rather than to your driveway, which requires many wheelbarrow loads to move it into the yard. If you don't have the option of bringing it closer to vehicular access, design the adjacent landscaping so you can wheel an oversized garden cart back and forth without restriction.

Dense soil (such as adobe, caliche, or hardpan) is very slow to absorb water, and if over irrigated, standing water can cause sensitive young plants to rot.

MITIGATION: Install a new gate in your fence or enlarge an existing one to facilitate future access.

Fencing

In yards accessible to wildlife, kids, and pets, a fence for your garden will be essential to its survival. If you must fence it against deer, the structure can be overwhelming. If this ele-

Bermuda grass is the scourge of gardens due to its dense root system and traveling stems that spread rapidly to infest soil with viable rootlets and seed.

ment has not been properly considered, the attempted solution may not only be unattractive, it may not solve the problem. Always take your time to design the right kind of protective barrier both above- and belowground, with consideration for its possible impact on the circulation of your backyard and the aesthetic of your landscaping.

MITIGATION: Design a fence that is both visually appealing and effective at keeping plant-eaters or destroyers out of your crops (see Chapter 6).

Simple peeler poles and a roll of small grid wire fencing keep pets and rodents out of the garden.

A rustic picket fence looks great and keeps pets and kids out, but small rodents such as ground squirrels can slide through the gaps to wreak havoc.

NIMBY Plants: Not in My Backyard

Trees that hail from dry climates around the world evolved a unique way of hoarding soil moisture. They literally make it impossible for other plants to grow beneath their canopies by exuding toxins into the soil that work like herbicides. In fact, the earliest herbicides were modeled after these botanical toxins. Plants that do this are called allelopathic; I call them NIMBYs.

Each species has its own toxin. The tamarisk is known as salt cedar, because it causes the soil around the tree to become super salty. Oils can leach out of fallen leaves as they decompose into the soil, as happens with oak and pine. A toxin can originate with fruits or husks of nuts, such as the tannic-acid-rich walnut. It even can come from bark and roots, as happens with eucalyptus. Beware if you have a NIMBY tree in your yard because soil beneath will contain toxins. The older the tree, the more toxic the soil.

COMMON NIMBY TREES

- Beefwood
  (Casuarina equisitifolia)

- Black Locust
  (Robinia pseudoacacia)

- Black Walnut
  (Juglans nigra)

- Eucalyptus
  (Eucalyptus spp.*)*

- Tree of Heaven
  (Ailanthus altissima)

Tree of heaven, Ailanthus altissima, *reduces competition for limited water supply with ailanthone.*

Australian eucalyptus can negatively influence soils beneath or around its canopy.

The accumulative litter beneath a tamarisk can significantly change soil with salt.

MITIGATION: Avoid creating a garden within the dripline of the canopy if you can, because these trees are also water hogs that root aggressively to find new sources. If there aren't any other suitable locations for your garden, create raised beds and line the bottoms with a barrier of weed-blocking fabric before you bring in new soil to fill them. This fabric allows water to drain through while preventing tree roots from accessing your imported soil. Keep tree litter from accumulating within your beds year round to prevent toxins from accumulating there.

THE DUST BOWL

Merciless winds tore up the soil that once gave the Southern Great Plains life and hurled it in roaring black clouds across the nation. Hopelessly indebted farmers fed tumbleweed to their cattle, and, in the case of one Oklahoma town, to their children. By the 1930s, years of injudicious cultivation had devastated 100 million acres of Kansas, Oklahoma, Texas, Colorado, and New Mexico.

—TIMOTHY EGAN

The Dust Bowl was the result of the most severe drought to ever hit the Midwest, but there was more to it than lack of rain. Much of this land was originally home to the prairie plant communities that fed the buffalo. Over eons, these deep-rooted grasses developed a thick layer of dead stems, roots, and leaves called sod, which was so dense it could be cut into bricks and stacked to make the first pioneer homes.

Fertile clay soils left dry and exposed can be easily taken up into great dust clouds due to the microscopic size of the soil particles.

Farmers had to strip away this thick layer to access some of the most fertile soils on Earth. Fed by the organic matter and microbes that thrived beneath the sod, this ground was dark and rich. At first there was little problem with stripping sod, but as more and more of it disappeared, millions of acres of soil were exposed to the drying forces of prairie winds. When drought struck in the 1930s, all that soil dried out so completely that it could easily be carried off by the hard-blowing prairie winds. These years would produce the Dust Bowl, when 300 million tons of ground soil was lost, resulting in the desertification of our nation's most fertile ground.

CONSIDERING WIND BARRIERS

Because a vegetable garden contains living plants, your wind barrier choice must be made with respect to their specific needs for air and light. However, you might find that less-expensive solutions are sometimes the best ones.

Block Wind, Not Light

Through the growing season, the sun's position will change, and in the desert, where many vegetables can be grown in winter when the sun is low in the southern sky, wind barriers can block much-needed morning or afternoon sun. When the wind comes from any direction but north, consider using translucent materials for your windscreen to allow the sun to shine through. Plexiglas or fiberglass panels make an excellent solid fence. Synthetic shade cloth is strong enough to reduce wind but designed to block only a percentage of the sun's rays.

The corrugated fiberglass panels used in this windscreen provide protection while maintaining a good deal of light penetration.

Minimize Support Structures

In areas with significant wind or where storm-driven wind can be extreme, a wind fence can easily blow over due to the load carried by the posts. Rather than sinking giant posts into concrete footings, consider using more porous windscreen materials such as 90 percent shade cloth, which diffuses the load. This material is used in the desert for controlling fugitive dust from construction sites. It's dense but some air can pass through, or it has cutouts at regular intervals so more wind passes through at specific points. This reduced wind load on the posts allows for less-expensive, lightweight materials that make installing posts an easy DIY project.

Preserve Air Movement

Using solid fences or walls to control wind can create problems in the garden. Pests such as whiteflies afflict greenhouse crops because there's little air movement within the greenhouse. Diseases such as mildew also thrive in stagnant air. Some air movement through the wind barrier is important to plant health.

Allow Seasonal Use

Sometimes wind problems occur only in certain seasons, or you are growing only part of the year where winters are cold, as they are in high mountain locations. The ability to easily remove a wind barrier for storage can be valuable, and can contribute to its longevity. Design a barrier that easily comes apart for storage. Use posts that slide into pipe sleeves buried in the ground and attach synthetic textile fabric with reusable fasteners so there will be nothing left behind to spoil your view.

Create a simple windscreen using lodgepole pine tree stakes and a sheet of shade cloth that can be set up or removed as conditions dictate.

PALM FROND FENCING FROM THE 29 PALMS INN

Wind in the desert can be hot and dry in the summer and cold and dry in the winter, so the gardeners at the 29 Palms Inn in the high desert northeast of Palm Springs, with its historic oasis grove of palm trees, developed their own unique wind fence out of recycled fronds. Anyone with a plethora of fronds can make a similar fence to shelter large areas without cutting off air movement. Here's how to do it:

1. Obtain a very thick pair of work gloves, because fan palms have ferocious barbs on their stems.

2. Gather green palm fronds with about 6 inches of stem or petiole attached.

3. Obtain a length of agricultural field fencing at a farm supply store or welded wire reinforcing mesh at a home improvement store.

4. Cut a section of fencing material to span about 6 to 8 feet between 4x4 wood posts, and lay it flat on the ground.

5. Tightly fold a fan-shaped frond, just like you would fold a fan. Starting at the grid opening that will be against the soil or an inch or two above, weave the frond upward into the grid opening and the ones above it. Continue along the fence, inserting fronds into the adjacent set of grids.

6. Keep working your way up the grid, overlapping the fronds just like a roofer until you've covered the entire span of the fence. The more you overlap the fronds, the more density and wind resistance you'll get.

7. Use stout U-shaped nails to fix the grid onto the post on one end, then stretch it tight and fasten to the other post.

8. Add more posts, fencing spans, and fronds as necessary to shield your entire garden.

A simply made palm frond wind-screen looks great, costs little, and may vary in height as desired.

Palm-frond fences can be easily taken down, rolled up, and stored to use in the future, moved to a new house, or saved for another season.

HEDGES, WINDROWS, AND SHELTERBELTS

In the past, living plants were the primary means of controlling wind. The problem with these traditional windrow applications in areas of little water is that they require their own irrigation. Plants also need space to mature and become effective, something most yards are too small to accommodate. But where sufficient water is available on large suburban or rural properties, a live plant screen is the best way to protect a large edible garden. There are three different scales to consider.

Hedge

This is a linear planting of shrubs, typically evergreens. If properly selected for mature size, hedges may grow naturally without shearing. Examples of drought-resistant evergreens for hot, dry climates include:

- Hopseed Bush (*Dodonaea viscosa*)
- Christmasberry/toyon (*Heteromeles arbutifolia*)
- Juniper (*Juniperus* spp.)
- Oleander (*Nerium oleander*)

Tightly spaced coniferous evergreens are the traditional windbreaks due to their natural drought resistance and dense branching.

Windrow

This is a linear planting of trees that is used to protect farmland and orchards from wind damage. Old desert farms utilized tamarisk trees from northern Africa for the early experiments with agriculture in windy areas. Later it was learned that a single mature tamarisk can consume up to 300 gallons of groundwater per day, so widespread planting was halted where groundwater is limited. Today the preferred windbreak trees for similar conditions in hot, dry regions include:

- Beefwood/she-oak (*Casuarina equisetifolia*)
- Tecate cypress (*Cupressus forbesii*)
- Aleppo pine (*Pinus halepensis*)

Shelterbelt

Designed for Midwestern prairie farms with unlimited space, this is a blend of shrubs and trees that is grouped into a much thicker arrangement designed to reduce and baffle wind that would be too strong for control by a windrow.

MITIGATING SOLAR EXPOSURE

Your morning newscast may include a UV Index for the day to come. The National Weather Service does the calculation, which ranges on a scale from 1 to 11. A rating of 2 means there's low danger to those with sensitive skin or eyes. A rating of 6 means there's high potential for sun damage typical of the average summer day. Throughout the western deserts the UV Index can max out at 11+, which is rated extreme, and may continue to be so for weeks on end.

If you're a vegetable plant that's evolved to withstand a 6 on the UV Index, it's easy to see why damage would occur at 11. Yet this is so common throughout the Southwest and the Great Basin that it's the chief factor that limits growing in midsummer. The only way to maintain plants through the hottest season is by providing artificial shade that diffuses sunlight but does not eliminate it.

Using Shade Cloth

In the depths of summer, the last thing a desert garden needs is more heat. If you can shelter your vegetables by providing shade, they'll live through this intense season, although growth slows or even stops during the extreme heat of July and August in the desert. Use a shade cloth or build a "shade house" to cover your garden. Large-scale growers have been using shade houses for decades to protect young seedlings from too much sun early in life. Shade houses also create a suitable environment for ferns and other shade-loving plants. However, because vegetables require full sun for health and production, shading them properly can be tricky.

Here are some ways to know if there's too much shade:

- Plants elongate and grow spindly; may fail to branch.
- Foliage may take on a yellowish cast as chlorophyll fades.
- Plants won't flower or, if they do, flowers are too sparse and fruit doesn't form.
- Pests and diseases flourish on weakened plants.

Choosing the Right Shade Cloth

Shade and air movement are both necessary to cool your vegetable garden, so the proper shade cloth, not poly sheeting, is important. Shade cloth is a synthetic knitted material that allows air and light to move through freely, whether it's hung on the west side of the garden to block direct afternoon sun, or overhead. Poly sheeting is a solid material that limits air movement. After sunset, heat rises up to allow cooler air to take its place. When the shading material is solid, that heat can't escape as easily, creating more stress for plants, so it is not wise to use poly sheeting.

It is also important to choose the suitable type of shade cloth. The type sold at home improvement stores blocks 80 to 90 percent of the UV light, which is useful for shading livestock, pets, and people, but it's far too much for plants. A much wider range of shade cloth densities, starting as low as 30 percent, is produced for agricultural use and available online or through a catalog (see Resources).

Try 30 percent shade cloth to shelter desert gardens from too much summer UV exposure. This cloth also is ideal for shading your seedlings sown at the end

Shade cloth can be used to reduce UV exposure overhead and to mitigate hard afternoon sun on the west side.

of summer for the fall root and leaf garden. Shade cloth doesn't decompose like burlap or other organic alternatives, so it lasts for many years.

Creating a shade structure for your garden requires lightweight poles you can buy from the same catalogs, but you can also use those favored by swap-meet sellers. After erecting the structure, order your shade cloth precut to fit it and edged with tape and grommet holes so it's easily attached to the framework with plastic zip ties or metal tie wire. This makes it easy to set up in late June and take down in early September to let the weaker sun of fall shine in.

GREENHOUSES

For small-scale home gardens in the desert or where wind, snow, or other problems make it difficult to grow outdoors, a greenhouse may prove the most ideal solution. Today's greenhouses can be a box-shaped affair or Quonset style. Box or "hobby" greenhouses work best in small spaces, but for larger family gardens, particularly in the desert, the Quonset style is recommended. Its rounded shape is more aerodynamic so there's less wind resistance. Sold as hoop houses or cold-frame greenhouses, these can extend the growing season and sometimes allow cultivation year around. Even if a greenhouse isn't heated, its shelter may mitigate freezing conditions enough to allow you to grow through the winter months.

A polyfilm or double-walled greenhouse cover is advisable. The best way to understand the difference in greenhouse covers is to compare them to windows in your house. Older single-pane

Simple connection fittings and lightweight galvanized pipe are used here in 10-by-10-foot units that can support custom-made seasonal shade cloth covers during the depths of summer.

TIP: The structure sold at the home-improvement store for a tarped carport kit will work nicely for shading a desert vegetable garden in the summer. Simply find one of the right size and order a 30 percent shade cloth cover with grommets to fit it. Use the original tarp cover's dimensions as the basis for your shade cloth panel.

In windy desert regions or anywhere else that wind is a problem, large greenhouses are the perfect way to grow food without battling wind and sun.

windows allow more exchange of heat and cold through the glass. Contemporary double-pane windows offer much greater insulation value. Greenhouses covered with more expensive double-walled material will retain more heat in winter and accumulate less heat inside over summer. Double-wall is more rip-resistant too, and guaranteed for 10 years, so the investment is worth it. If you decide to use a heater, double-wall offers far more efficient insulation.

Growing vegetables in difficult climates, or cultivating them where there's limited water, requires attention to the environment. You can't depend on Mother Nature to create ideal conditions for these plants that have very specific needs and limitations. Fortunately, new ways to arrange our gardens and modern advances in outdoor textile manufacturing allow us to control a variety of issues, from water consumption to wind damage, desiccation, and high UV exposure. If gardeners learned one or all of these technologies, both ancient and modern, to grow food in a harsh climate, everyone could help to conserve water without giving up the dream of an organic garden-based lifestyle.

CHAPTER 3

Methods

Every garden is different, and yours will be unique to your taste, lifestyle, and location. Everyone can grow vegetables; it's just how much you can grow that varies. A single pot on the fire escape may grow a single tomato plant, with perhaps basil tucked in too. As you add more diversity and more quantity, it takes more water. Therefore the equation must be a unique balance that works for you and your family.

This chapter lays out your options according to the scale of your operation and details the best tips for getting the most out of your available space.

CONTAINERS: PORCH, PATIO, BALCONY

It's easier than you think to grow vegetables in containers, and this approach is perfect for those who live in apartments, condos, and town houses and lack access to an in-ground garden. Container gardening is an age-old practice that is evolving with new technology that helps improve productivity from small spaces. Above all, container growing is one of the most efficient techniques for water conservation.

TIP: If you are recycling black plastic nursery pots to use for growing vegetables, make sure they are pathogen-free each time they are replanted. Scrub the pot clean and then dip in a 10 percent bleach solution or spray the solution over all interior pot surfaces to kill microbes and diseases that could increase in numbers to infect your next crop.

Basic Containers

During times of little rain, growing vegetables in ordinary pots can be the most efficient of all means of cultivation. While it's long been traditional to use clay pots, they are heavy and easily broken. Plus, unglazed clay is designed to allow air and water exchange through the pot walls. That may be ideal for growing orna-

Winter greens are among the best vegetables to grow in traditional pots.

Moss baskets were originally designed for moisture-loving plants that need free drainage. They aren't recommended for growing food in hot, dry climates because the water you apply can rapidly evaporate, particularly when it's windy.

mental plants, but this water loss is not desirable when growing short-term vegetable crops during drought or in dry climates. Case in point: commercial nurseries universally choose black plastic nursery pots for growing plants long-term and keeping water costs minimal. They typically use drip irrigation, which, combined with the solid plastic pot walls, ensures optimal water use.

The best containers for serious vegetable growers are nursery pots because these are created for excellent drainage that prevents oversaturated root zones. Larger vegetable plants such as peppers need a sizable root zone, but not a super-deep one. While 15-gallon pots are designed to grow woody trees and shrubs, the ideal size for food crops is a 5-gallon pot. This provides enough room for a sizable root zone with sufficient moisture-holding capacity.

The Self-Watering Container: More Food, Less Space

Large-scale hydroponics revolutionized our ability to grow tons of food in a few square feet of space with the self-watering container (SWC). This new way to grow food blends container gardening with hydroponics for superior yields grown in the most water-conservative manner. It's a perfect problem solver for hot, dry climates due to the hydroponic design that keeps plants hydrated even in the most trying, arid places. If you are planning to grow a single tomato or twenty of them in pots, start here before taking another step toward traditional containers.

Each of these Grow Box self-watering containers supports two large tomato plants in just a few square feet on the pool deck.

The SWC come in a kit with soil and nutrients enough for a vigorous garden. Each SWC trough is about 1 foot by 2 feet in size, which fits more efficiently into smaller spaces than round pots do. Inside, the soil lies only in the top two-thirds of the container, on top of a perforated divider. The space in the bottom is a water reservoir. There's a standpipe open at the top or a side opening where you pour in water to fill the reservoir. This is ideal for secondhand clean, soap-free kitchen water.

This arrangement allows roots to grow through the soil and then the divider to ultimately trail naked in the reservoir, where they can drink up as much as they need each day. Fully enclosed, the water is not subject to much evaporation so that every drop is used by the plants. This arrangement also allows you to pack many plants into the trough because they don't have to compete for moisture. There are two leading brands selling the SWC. See Resources (page 191) to find manufacturers or buy online.

TIP: Those who grow in containers must always be conscious of the combined weight of the pot, its soil mass, and the water you apply. Together this may strain a wood deck, fire escape, or rooftop. Be aware that pots can stain surfaces beneath them, so it's best to invest in a wheeled trolley to facilitate cleaning and movement to maximize solar exposure during transitional seasons.

IT'S EASY TO PLANT A
SELF-WATERING CONTAINER

1. Self-watering containers are composed of two parts: the upper potting soil zone and a lower water reservoir.

2. Once assembled, fill the upper half with potting soil and plant seed or seedlings.

3. Once planted, lay out the surface pad with its nutrient pack and cut it to fit your planting arrangement.

4. The planted container is self-sufficient except for refilling the reservoir, which becomes a more frequent requirement as plants grow larger and need more moisture.

5. Simply insert your garden hose into the fill slot to top off the reservoir and begin the wicking process that feeds plants until their roots grow long enough to reach the water underneath.

My self-watering containers planted with store-bought tomato seedlings at the end of February in unheated greenhouse.

GOOD, BAD, AND UGLY: POTTING SOIL SELECTION

Potting soil companies focus on drainage, and sometimes this is achieved at the expense of fertility. Fast-draining soils often contain a high amount of perlite, which are those little white granules that look like bits of popcorn. These soils contain a high amount of undecomposed woody matter too, which looks like wood shavings. These materials don't pack down to keep the soil porous, so water travels through and out the bottom fast—sometimes too fast—compromising water-holding capacity. Over time the finer material will filter down and out of the drain holes with each watering, leaving behind a not-too-fertile root zone.

In dry conditions, drainage is often a secondary concern to water-holding capacity because evaporation rates can be so high. For this reason, you'll get much better results with pricier, quality potting soils that are more absorbent, holding the moisture you apply rather than speeding it to the drain holes. Those that contain a high amount of peat or coir, a by-product of coconut processing, will prove the best for maximized water-holding capacity. To take the guesswork out of the process, look for brands that promise improved water-holding capacity, such as Waterhold Cocoblend Potting Soil.

TIP: Weight is often the best way to know the proportion of perlite and woody matter in a potting soil. Both are very lightweight materials that make the product cheaper for the manufacturer to ship. Compare the weights of competing brands to evaluate the relative amounts of porous filler material in each.

RAISED BEDS: TIDY GARDENS FOR MODEST SPACES

Years ago, the only raised beds you'd see were in neighborhoods where soils were problematic. These problems can be natural, such as a limestone layer just below thin surface soils, or man-made, a result of cut-and-fill grading to create a building pad on a hillside, which removes the topsoil to expose heavy clays or chalk layers. Some low-lying areas in valleys can even be too salty, being in a location where an ancient lake dried up. In all these cases, growing vegetables in the ground requires raised beds and imported fill soil.

The surface roots of this old cypress tree made it impossible to grow vegetables in the ground, but creatively designed raised beds not only solve the problem but also look great when viewed from second-story windows.

ON THE UP AND UP MAY BE A DOWNER

Vertical gardening is hot at the moment, but the amount of moisture it needs is not. At least some of the vertical gardening systems are water-guzzlers because they are so vulnerable to evaporation due to soil exposed to air. For example, in dry conditions the fabric pocket systems suspended on walls can be problematic because their permeability, designed to enhance drainage, also causes moisture to evaporate through the material quickly. In hot, dry climates, wind can dry them out in a matter of hours. It takes twice as much water to keep the soil moist enough for vegetable plants to grow, which is totally counterproductive.

TIP: The rectangular shape of the self-watering containers can be adapted to vertical growing in narrow spaces when used with a wall trellis to support vining plants such as pole beans and cucumbers.

In climates with dry heat and no summer rainfall, only systems professionally installed with strong hydroponic technology will survive. These systems are expensive and sometimes unpredictable. The idea may work great until the first heat wave, and then reality sets in. It's best to try this on a small scale first to determine whether your location and exposure can support it before making a grand investment.

Blinded by Beauty: Aesthetics versus Problem Solving

Before you proceed with creating raised beds, give some serious thought to why you're making them. What you do for aesthetic reasons can be vastly different from practical solutions to problems. The costs can be widely different as well.

Raised beds are too often created just because somebody likes the way they look. What they're really after is a rigid edge or defined limits of a planting space, not true raised beds. Aesthetic beds are created with a simple boundary board of some sort and a few inches of imported soil over natural ground. Plant roots will, over the course of the season, penetrate well beyond the new soil. This is desirable because plants supported by just a thin layer of rich soil won't fare well with low-water gardening. The thin top layer causes the plant to develop a shallow root zone that results in perpetual problems with wilt, pests, and diseases.

Problem-solving raised beds are another matter entirely. These are created to provide a full root zone to the plants because the soil underneath isn't suitable. Therefore, their depth must be significantly greater, which leads to much greater costs early on. A 2-foot-deep raised bed must have strong sidewalls to hold not only the imported the soil, but the additional weight of water in that soil, which adds about 8 pounds per gallon. And then there's the cost of obtaining a truckload of topsoil to fill it, or the effort of carting around umpteen bags of potting soil.

> **TIP:** Just because you grow in ground doesn't mean you can't have lovely old-fashioned layouts in geometric shapes. In fact, each year you can devise a new shape for planting. To better define these shapes, use recycled wood and stake it in place for the season to line walking areas, then remove the boards and stakes in the spring to easily till the entire space before planting next year.

When the soil is so unsuitable or when there are problems with it (such as root knot nematodes), plants must rely strictly on imported soil.

Raised Beds in the Desert

Desert animals often bury themselves in the sand to escape the heat of the day. This may have first inspired Pueblo gardeners in the Southwest to drop the level of their planting squares to better use the soil mass to keep roots cooler. These examples suggest that raising beds in this environment may not be the best idea.

Raised beds made of masonry are the best choice for heat and drought due to their longevity and thickness that insulates roots from absorbing heat through the bed walls during the day.

TIP: Before landscape contractors pour a sidewalk or patio, they often lay a sleeve in the ground underneath the slab. This allows pipes and electrical wire to be threaded under the paving at a future date. When creating your raised beds, lay sleeves to connect them using 2-inch or 3-inch diameter polyethylene drain line underneath the walking surfaces to allow your irrigation to be piped invisibly from one raised planter to the next. Sleeves are cheap insurance that your design today will adapt to your growing needs tomorrow.

Any time you raise the soil mass above grade, it has three results: First, the root zone loses its earthen protection from direct solar exposure, as sun on the raised bed causes the soil mass to overheat. Second, the plants are raised up above grade where they are more exposed to drying winds. Third, water applied to overheated soil may evaporate far more quickly.

So how do we solve soil problems that prevent typical in-ground growing? Split the difference by combining a small raised edge of 6 inches with another 6 inches of excavated native soil to create a good-sized, 12-inch-deep zone of imported potting soil or topsoil. This provides the tidy look of a raised bed with the insulating benefits from the surrounding soil.

Few Options for Caliche and Kin

Caliche, or hardpan, is present in some desert home sites and heavy clays that defy drainage are found elsewhere as well. Growing anything in these soils is nearly impossible, because even when broken up, caliche will return to its original density after the first irrigation or rain due to a natural chemical reaction. Very fine clays such as adobe are dense they take on the characteristics of potter's clay. Called "plastic" soils, these are difficult to till when wet and impossible to dig when dry. Raised beds that are 100 percent above the natural soil are the best solution for growing vegetables under these conditions.

METALS ARE HOT

Cor-ten steel is one of the swankiest raised bed wall materials used in upscale homes and gardens. It doesn't rot like wood and is literally tough as iron. While Cor-ten's ability to absorb heat may be beneficial in northern climates, in the desert it can actually cook your vegetables before they reach the kitchen. When sun strikes metal surfaces they absorb heat very quickly, and if you doubt this, just touch a car hood on a hundred-degree day. Yes, you can fry an egg on it. When this occurs with metal raised beds, the heat is absorbed and transferred to the soil mass, which gets far hotter than it should. This in turn stimulates surface evaporation and literally cooks the roots. In the desert when temperatures can easily exceed 105 to 110 degrees F for weeks at a time, that soil mass becomes an oven. Moreover, the heat absorbed in the steel continues to be released into the raised bed at night. During late night and early morning hours, soils should be cooling, but metal raised beds can interfere with this, denying the plants the nocturnal benefit they need.

TIP: Beware of using corrugated metal roofing or galvanized stock water tanks for raised beds in the desert. Though they don't get as hot as dark Cor-ten, they will reach the temperature of a car hood every single day.

Consider Material Life Span

Virtually any kind of wood can be used to construct raised beds, but beware: these beds are not permanent. Contractors know that any wood that has direct contact with earth will soon rot away through natural processes. This means that the soil and moisture inside a raised bed soil triggers the decomposition process from day one. The only way to slow this process is to line raised beds with a waterproof membrane. Not only does the membrane increase longevity of the bed, it also helps maintain soil moisture. This is just like the difference between an unglazed clay pot and a plastic nursery pot, with one allowing moisture through the walls while the other retains it. Keep this in mind, because water retention is important if using wooden raised beds.

Woods such as railroad ties and landscape timbers contain chemical wood preservatives to slow decomposition. Some organic gardeners will not consider these products due to their chemical content, though risks are minimal. Pallet wood is often untreated, and though popular as a recycled material, it can rot in the first or second year, proving this is not a good choice.

Porous woods such as redwood and cedar naturally resist decomposition and have long been used for water storage tanks. Their porosity is engineered into the tank's construction. When first built, a tank may leak, but once each stave absorbs a lot of water and expands, the gaps close. If the water level drops for any period of time and the staves are fully exposed, they will dry out and the gaps will return. Therefore, remember that porous woods will experience perpetual moisture evaporation from the outside surfaces, which does help to keep the contents cooler, but over time this process will contribute to water loss.

COMPARING RAISED BED WALL MATERIALS

MATERIAL	COST	LONGEVITY	WATER-HOLDING POTENTIAL	TOXICITY
Composite	High	Longer	Low	None
Redwood	High	Long	High	None
Cedar	Medium/high	Long	Medium	None
Railroad tie	Low	Long	Low	Varies
Concrete block	High	Longest	High	Alkaline*
Poured concrete	High	Longest	High	Alkaline*

*Concrete products contain lime, which gradually leaches into the adjacent soil with the water you apply. The minerals in the lime, which include a variety of salts, accumulate over time. This causes neutral soil to gradually become more alkaline (at the salty end of the pH scale). Though it's not an immediate issue, knowing it can happen over time, particularly where the water supply is already on the alkaline side, helps you diagnose problems with plant health along the edges of these raised beds where soil directly contacts concrete.

Composite Lumber: Tough and Sustainable

Composite lumber is a green product made from recycled plastic that is almost rot-proof. This material does well in the desert and makes excellent raised beds that hold up over time despite the extremes of temperature and UV exposure. There are many different brands and they vary in cost, but higher-end products will be more reliable for this application due to the amount of UV exposure raised beds receive. Also note that composite lumber is heavier than standard lumber and may require a different support arrangement, which may be an issue if the beds are being created as containers upon an existing structure. Beware of plastic corner connector longevity in the desert environment as well. Seek out metal corner connectors or skip the corner pieces and just build with wood screws for more secure connections.

I NEVER THOUGHT OF THAT!

When deciding whether to use raised beds or plant your garden in a ground-level bed, consider these issues:

When using more than one raised bed, it's important to plan for irrigation lines. Lay sleeves to connect them underground.

This in-ground garden features the ancient four-square design of European gardens.

1. If you want to use a rototiller to work amendments into the raised-bed soil, you will need a small rototiller, so you can lift it up into taller raised beds.

2. Raised beds require you purchase a large amount (L x W x H = volume) of potting soil or topsoil, haul it to your house, and deliver it to the backyard. That's a lot of money and labor. If your natural soil is suitable, why not save that money for top-notch amendments to build up healthy, organic native soil and grow its microbe populations.

3. The ability to rotate crops is crucial to natural pest and disease control. Very small beds may develop problems because there isn't enough room to rotate your tomatoes sufficiently to ensure there's no build-up of the diseases that plague these plants.

4. Consider how you'll set up your drip irrigation system in raised beds. The tubing will have to go across the walking surfaces between beds to connect them to the water source.

Failure to accommodate the irrigation design when laying out the raised beds often results in unnecessary water or pressure losses.

IN GROUND

Growing vegetables in natural soil is the most rewarding, flexible, and affordable way to go. Unless you're faced with problematic ground such as caliche, heavy clay, bedrock, or parent material, most soils—even those in the desert—can become fertile ground for vegetables. Today, many folks new to vegetable gardening soon find their pots and raised beds too limiting and yearn to spread out into a larger space. In-ground home gardens have fed Americans from colonial times through the Great Depression, and Victory Gardens kept fresh food on many children's plates during World War II. The simple, backyard, in-ground garden is the workhorse of family nutrition.

RAINWATER HARVESTING

Using a rain barrel or even an underground cistern to catch and store rainwater are great ways to reduce your dependence on city water. A rain barrel is typically located at the rain gutter downspouts, while cisterns are often much larger. When setting up the barrel or cistern, consider a piped delivery system at the same time. Unless you have an ideally sloping lot with your vegetable garden at a lower elevation, you may find it challenging or labor-intensive to use the stored water on vegetables located in ground or in raised beds. If you don't have an ideal gravity-flow situation, a small pump close to the house sends water to the vegetable garden without manual labor. This demonstrates why it is important to consider how you will deliver your harvested water when conceiving the new garden's size, location, and layout.

Power Tillage Makes Cents

An in-ground garden is the domain of the rototiller. It saves more time and money than any other tool you'll ever buy. If you'll only use it once a year at planting time, renting one for a half or whole day to accomplish the task is the ideal solution. Plus, the rental yard makes sure it starts and is in top condition. Big, strong tillers are a must for large gardens, particularly where there are rocks present. These machines are excellent investments that increase the range and success of a family garden, because they allow you to:

- Open up dense ground to increase ease and depth of water penetration to maximize accessibility to roots.

- Work up remnant roots, bark, and wood when developing a new garden area.

- Turn under winter weeds prior to spring planting.

- Mix in compost, manure, fertilizers, and other soil amendments in spring and fall.

- Quickly change crops from cool season to warm season and back again in the fall.

- Work in remnants of last year's plants.

Gas-powered rototillers are work-horses, particularly in heavy clay soils or those with rocks.

Small gardens and raised beds with easy-to-work, rock-free soil can take advantage of electric tillers.

Sizing Your Garden

New gardeners often ask how big they should make their beds. The answer is, as big as it needs to be.

If you're growing pumpkins that demand lots of space, you'll need a lot of ground. Ditto winter squash and melons. If you just want tomatoes and a few peppers, then less area is required. The chief benefit of having a large in-ground garden is for crop rotation. Space allows you to put each crop on fresh ground every year. When a crop is grown in the same place for several consecutive years, pests and diseases build up to damaging levels. Even if you don't plant the entire garden each year, those areas you leave fallow still benefit from a periodic rest that helps increase fertility.

Terraces: Super Slope Solutions

If your lot is on a gentle slope, it's important to level the ground where you'll be growing. This is the ancient art of making terraces for growing, just as it was in the Andes where the first potatoes were planted. A terrace ensures that water penetrates downward into the root zone instead of running off before it can benefit plants. Sloping ground also loses its most fertile surface soils when rain causes erosion, carrying away particles in the runoff. It's quite simple to terrace a garden using timbers, tree trunks, or railroad ties staked into place with rebar on the lower edge of a terrace. This method is not cut-and-fill grading but a build up of the lower edge of each terrace with imported topsoil. The depth of each terrace is governed by the degree of slope and the height of your timber.

Everyone has the opportunity to enjoy homegrown organic produce, no matter where you live. Success is deeply rooted in understanding the limitations of extreme climates and exploiting new and innovative opportunities for water harvesting. Whether your solutions are simple or complex, they are all based on the same universal concepts and a knowledge base honed through the span of time. Whether you grow one fabulous tomato on a balcony or create the quintessential family garden in the backyard, when you plan creatively for growth without excessive water use, everybody wins.

CHAPTER 4

Build Organic Soil

*The soil is not, as many suppose, a dead, inert substance.
It is very much alive and dynamic. It teems with bacteria, actinomycetes, fungi, molds, yeasts, protozoa, algae
and other minute organisms.*

—J. I. RODALE, *PAY DIRT*

As organic gardeners, we don't feed the plants, we feed the soil. Rodale knew this in 1959 and it is still the backbone of organic gardening today. Plants that grow in rich, biologically active soils gain a greater ability to withstand drought or extreme heat. The organisms in these soils contain microbes that can enter the plants to improve the uptake of soil moisture and fortify the immune system.

When growing vegetables with minimal water use, plant health is essential. We know that plants that are "poor doers" due to problems such as nutrient deficiency are the first to experience pests and diseases. This is because their immune systems have been compromised. When we ask water-loving vegetables to perform on a diet, their needs must be met in every other way to help them withstand these rigors. Therefore, the most important part of what you do in low-water vegetable gardening to support plants is to build bio-intensive soils and maintain them.

MICROBES

A wide range of microscopic organisms that live in soil, feed on organic matter, and offer many benefits to plants.

HUMUS

A finely textured material, such as finished compost, resulting from organic matter consumed in the decomposition process. Humus can hold up to 80 percent of its weight in moisture.

The desert is notorious for lean soils that are often sandy, gravelly ground with little or no organic matter. This lack of humus means that there is little to no food for microbes, so few survive in desert soil. The absence of moisture over long periods discourages microbes as well. Therefore, there is no way for organic matter to naturally decompose in these soils because microbes are essential to this process. As a result, desert soils experience a perfect storm of deficiencies that render them infertile, unable to hold water, and nearly devoid of microbial life. Therefore, rehabilitating lean desert soils to make them bioactive can be a big challenge that takes a long time, tons of amendments, and the introduction of microbes.

STRUCTURE

The relative percentages of sand, silt, and clay in your soil. Sand will be the most porous and easy to work, clay will be the densest. Soil structure is crucial to how the water you apply behaves within the soil and whether it drains properly.

Common problems with desert soil and solutions for building it:

Problem: Porous soils lack cohesiveness.
Solution: Introduce a wide range of different types of organic matter to bind particles.

Problem: Porous soils lack water-holding capacity.
Solution: Introduce fine humus to act as mini-sponges to increase absorbency.

Problem: Porous soils lack microbes.
Solution: Introduce microbe-rich manures and concentrated bio-products.

Problem: Porous soils are vulnerable to nutrient deficiencies.
Solution: Apply generous amounts of organic fertilizers and worm castings.

Only well-adapted desert natives thrive in the eroded soils and sandy dry washes.

SIMPLE TEST FOR DRAINAGE

Knowing your soil drainage isn't just about observing what happens on top. It's what's going on deeper down that has the biggest impact on how plants use water and how fast it drains through, or doesn't. Very dense, deeper layers can spell trouble in vegetable gardens, but you won't know a dense layer is there unless you know how to test for it. The best way is to dig a test hole. In the process, you'll see the "soil horizon," which is a cross-section of the underground edge made visible by the excavation. The horizon reveals different soil layers and the actual depth of your topsoil, the most fertile ground.

ORGANIC MATTER

A wide range of matter derived from plants and animals. When added to soil, microbes break it down into a simpler form utilized by living plants.

Here is how to perform the test:

1. Dig a hole about 2 feet deep at the center of the garden area.

2. Fill it with water.

3. Observe how much time it takes for water to drain from the hole.

- If it drains within an hour, you have great drainage.

- If it takes a day to drain, drainage is slow.

- If it takes longer than a day to drain, you have a drainage problem.

AVOID WOODY MATTER

Not all organic matter is the same, and wood chips or woody fragments can be downright problematic in your soil. When you add non-decomposed woody matter like chips or shavings directly to your soil, the microbes underground must work very hard to break it down. To do so, they derive energy from the nitrogen existing in your soil. As they do their job, the nitrogen demand can actually deplete fertility in the immediate area. So while you think you're adding all this fertile organic matter to your garden, it's actually degrading fertility.

Often woody matter is used to open up clay soil for improved drainage. Redwood soil amendment (RSA) was used for this purpose because redwood is naturally resistant to decay and keeps clay draining much longer than other types of wood. While solving one problem, this extended resistance actually created another: nitrogen deficiency. For this reason, gardeners began adding extra nitrogen fertilizer with RSA to compensate for the loss.

The same is true when using manures mixed with wood shavings used as livestock bedding. These manures are quite low in nitrogen so there's not enough to compensate for the losses. When using this kind of material to improve water-holding capacity in sandy soils or to keep clay draining in your vegetable garden, add organic nitrogen fertilizers such as alfalfa meal, blood meal, or guano.

Shredded palm fronds and stems can be used for surface mulch, but palm matter actually resists decomposition. That means it is not suited as a soil amendment, but it will make a long-lasting surface mulch.

Organic matter from palms is best used only as mulch.

Palms are the dominant trees in many desert communities and warm climate regions, so you'd think they provide tons of organic matter for gardens. Wrong. Desert palm fronds are highly resistant to decomposition. Native fan palms retain their "skirt" of dead fronds for life, which can be a century or more. It explains why they're so popular as roofing thatch in Mexico. Grinding them up in a shredder doesn't work because fronds contain such strong fibers that they clog the mechanism. The only solution is to cut them into tiny, confetti-like bits, which is time-consuming and hard on your hands. Then work the fragments into very wet organic matter to drive decomposition. The compost heap must remain consistently moist enough for this to work over the long term. On the other hand, this resistance to decomposition makes chopped palm frond waste a perfect mulch. There's more on mulches and how they work at the end of this chapter. Also see Chapter 2 on creating a useful wind barrier with woven wire fencing and palm fronds.

TEAMING WITH MICROBES

The most important reading for organic gardeners is *Teaming With Microbes: The Organic Gardener's Guide to the Soil Food Web* by Jeff Lowenfels and Wayne Lewis. This very-well-illustrated hardcover book, published in 2010, is a scientific overview of many different kinds of soil microbes, including bacteria, fungi, algae, protozoa, and nematodes. This book was first made popular among hydroponic growers who are challenged to provide everything

> **MYCORRHIZAE**
>
> Fungal organisms that actually enter the roots of plants to live symbiotically for the benefit of both. One type of mycorrhizae, often called the "inoculant," allows leguminous plants to utilize atmospheric nitrogen and transfer it into the soil.

a plant needs in their sterile means of cultivation. In many ways, granular desert soils are similar to hydroponic growing media, so much of what you read in this book is ideal for facing these challenges.

MIRACULOUS MYCORRHIZAE

Mycorrhizae is one of the most important areas of research for increasing drought resistance in plants and improving production of agricultural crops. There are many different species of mycorrhizae; some are endophytes that live within the root and some are ectophytes that live on the outside of it. Each strain is associated with different kinds of plants. Much research is ongoing in the effort to use this biotechnology to improve drought resistance, which can give your garden the edge in drought and improve water use. There are many small companies online that are producing easy-to-use inoculant you can buy to add resilience to your crops. These inoculants originated to serve the home hydroponic industry but are proving great problem solvers for enhancing food production in difficult climates. Here's how mycorrhizae work in water conservation:

- They expand the roots by adding their own expansive network of absorbing strands to mine the soil for water and the dissolved minerals carried there.

- They influence the opening or closing of the "stomata," the breathing pores in leaves. Under drought stress the plant closes its stomata to reduce water loss.

- They increase water pressure or "turgor" in plant tissues to prevent or delay wilt.

PROBIOTICS FOR POOR OR DEPLETED SOILS

If you're cultivating depleted soils such as sandy desert ground, or are gardening on subsoils after topsoil was graded away, microbe populations may be minimal. Many forms of organic soil amendments such as compost, manures, and guano contain loads of microbes. Using these organic fertilizers and amendments is the best way to increase populations significantly, but this takes time. There are more concentrated products that work like probiotics for your soil to speed and diversify population growth. Simply spread it around the garden and work it in to start new populations.

Just remember that once you've introduced them to the soil, you must feed them with quality compost and manures to keep the populations alive and growing. Be generous with compost when you inoculate your garden to get them off to a good start and keep adding new amendments each year to maintain effectiveness.

The most widely available products are compost starters designed to be used in compost heaps to increase decomposition rates. More focused, general bio-enriched products, like Dr. Earth's Super Active Natural and Organic Biological Soil Inoculant, aren't as easy to find but work equally well. To import mycorrhizae for increased pea and bean production, select a product like Chappy's Power Organics Root Booster Myco Inoculant.

KELP: A NATURAL PLANT STEROID FOR DROUGHT RESISTANCE

Fish emulsion has always been the liquid fertilizer of choice for organic gardeners. Liquid plant foods are better for dry and desert gardens because limited moisture means pelleted or dry fertilizer products dissolve too slowly. Without enough water, they can't be carried into the root zone, but diluted fish emulsion travels quickly into the soil for much easier and more immediate uptake.

Many swear by this fertilizer by-product of the fishing industry due to consistently superior performance despite the relatively low nitrogen content (just 2 percent). In recent years, that mystery was solved by science. Researchers discovered that fish emulsion contains a good deal of kelp. This marine plant contains high concentrations of cytokinins, which are plant growth hormones. They are akin to steroids that help build muscle in humans. Kelp inadvertently integrated with fishing by-products was bringing cytokinins into the root zone of plants, where it was stimulating cell division. Plants fed with fish emulsion therefore were performing better. This tells us that vegetable plants everywhere can reap big benefits from fish emulsion. Better yet, use straight kelp fertilizer in liquid form. Adding this concentration of kelp helps your plants recover from wilt more easily and produce a much larger root system that is able to reach deeper to access more soil moisture during hot or very dry periods.

MICRONUTRIENTS

These nutrients are needed for plant growth but in much smaller amounts; sometimes just a trace is required. The most important are boron, chlorine, copper, iron, manganese, molybdenum, and zinc.

MACRONUTRIENTS

The three chief macronutrients in soil are nitrogen, phosphorus, and potassium. Nitrogen is responsible for stem and leaf growth and is vital to leaf crops. Phosphorus and potassium are linked to roots, flowers, and fruit production vital to most vegetable plants.

SOIL AMENDMENTS AND FERTILIZERS

There's a lot of confusion over the differences between soil amendments and fertilizers. This is because some soil additives function as both. Generally speaking, soil amendments are used to feed microbes and change soil structure, making heavy clays open up to drain and binding sandy ground to help it hold water. Fertilizers are nutritionally important materials that bring macro- and micronutrients into the root zone for easy uptake by plants, but these may not influence soil structure at all. Compost is so highly valued because it functions as an amendment and fertilizer by simultaneously improving soil structure, introducing nutrients, and feeding microbes. Virtually all top soil amendments are the same in that they contain organic matter, but what divides them is the source of that material and the degree of decomposition.

Fish emulsion is an excellent liquid-based fertilizer that produces quick results in dry gardens because it's mixed with water and poured onto the root zone. This makes it immediately available to plants whereas dry organic fertilizers need microbes and moisture to break materials down before they are available to plants.

TIP: Adding the hormones in kelp and the endophytes of mycorrhizae are the two most effective ways to increase drought resistance in plants. Consider them the probiotics of the vegetable garden that naturally pump up plant resilience.

Compost

Whether you make it at home or purchase it in bags, this material is considered the most beneficial to vegetable gardens. Compost can be variable, though, so beware of some off-brands that may not be up to par. Rule of thumb: the more diverse its origins, the richer a compost will be.

Composted Manure

Because animal manure can contain seeds of noxious and invasive weeds, it should be composted so the heating process kills most, if not all, seeds. Consider poultry manure the strongest, steer manure the most affordable, and horse manure the lowest in fertility. Beware of inadequately composted horse manure because, with only one stomach, these animals do not digest weed seeds as well as cattle with three stomachs.

Soil Conditioner

This term refers to a variety of products used to improve your soil when added before or during planting season. Quality can vary considerably, and many contain high amounts of forest industry by-products. Beware of soil conditioners containing too much undecomposed woody matter unless you are trying to amend heavy clay. Even then, be sure to add fertilizer to maintain overall nitrogen levels.

Planter Mix

This is another nonspecific term used to describe mixtures of organic matter often used when planting trees and shrubs. Some planter mixes contain composted biosolids, which may not be desirable for food-producing gardens.

It makes sense to make compost at home using all sorts of organic waste materials from house and garden.

Peat Amendments

Ground peat has long been the primary ingredient of soil conditioners and planter mixes to improve water-holding capacity. Environmental concerns over sustainability of peat resources has led to increased use of coir, a by-product of the coconut-processing industry. Using peat in dry climates is problematic because once peat dries out, it resists rehydration.

In desert regions, low or nonexistent humidity radically slows or periodically stops decomposition, so use a fully enclosed composter to maintain even moisture.

RENEWABLE COIR TO THE RESCUE!

Coir is a real drought buster! This sustainable, green product is the hottest new replacement for dwindling peat resources and is particularly useful during drought. This by-product of the coconut-processing industry is composed of the fibrous husk of coconut ground into a fine compost-like consistency. Coir can absorb nine times its weight in water, so when used as an amendment during drought, it keeps the soil around plant roots more evenly moist over a longer period between water applications. While coir offers no nutritional value, it is the ideal way to open clay soils and add water-holding capacity to sand. Using coir in average soil helps reduce the frequency of water applications, thereby reducing overall water use naturally.

ORGANIC FERTILIZERS

When you're trying to build up lean soils to benefit plants in drought, it is crucial to select organic fertilizers strong enough to get the job done. Fertilizer is gauged by three numbers that indicate the percentage of nitrogen, phosphorus, and potassium (N-P-K) present in the product. The larger the number, the more potent it is. These numbers will seem very low compared to synthetic fer-

Planter mix may look like potting soil, but the lack of white perlite proves it's not. Note the amount of raw woody matter present, which lightens clay soils but may reduce fertility if not augmented with nitrogen fertilizer.

tilizers used on turf and ornamental gardens, where they become available to plants instantly but move out of the root zone just as quickly. Organic fertilizers take longer to interact with soils and become available to plant roots, but once they do, these remain beneficial for an extended time. It's more than just the nutrients at play here, because during drought, organic fertilizers offer many other benefits such as micronutrients, microbes, and trace elements that enhance a plant's immune system and ability to come back after wilt.

FARMING WITH FORMULATED FERTILIZERS

Diversity is key when selecting organic fertilizers because the more wide-ranging the sources of nutrients, the more beneficial they are to bio-active soils. Formulated fertilizers come pre-blended under various brand names, such as Dr. Earth or Black Gold. Choose those designated for food plants to obtain the optimal blend. This is far more affordable than using individual elements such as alfalfa meal. Apply organic fertilizers generously because they won't burn like synthetic fertilizers do. Think ahead and work fertilizers into your soil well before your planting date so they have enough time to become fully active and available for young plants to use them. Adding fertilizer at planting time may delay its benefits for well over a month in drier conditions.

MULCH: THE ULTIMATE DROUGHT BUSTER

While fertilizers and amendments are used to improve soil structure and fertility, mulches are the workhorses of the dry garden. They're composed of any kind of bulk organic material that's spread over the top of the soil, where it acts much like a protective umbrella. Mulch is the most powerful tool in maximizing the benefit of water you apply.

- Mulch shades the ground like insulation to keep soil and roots cooler in the heat.
- Mulch blocks direct solar exposure on the soil surface to prevent surface evaporation.
- Mulch blocks sunlight from reaching the soil to prevent weed growth.

The most common type of vegetable garden mulch is straw because it's cheap and easily transported in bales. Anything locally available, such as shredded leaves or wood chips, works equally well. Chips may be obtained from green waste programs, but beware that some sources of wood chips may include material from allelopathic trees such as eucalyptus and black walnut. These leaves leach toxic chemicals into the soil that are damaging to vegetable plants. See details on these problem trees in Chapter 2.

Mulches that resist decomposition are not tilled into the soil because there is no nutrient value. At the end of the season, rake them up, set aside, and reuse next year.

FERTILIZERS AND MANURE POTENCY GUIDE

These charts help you see at a glance which fertilizers are the powerhouses of the organic world. It also shows why you must use so much more of it to achieve the same N-P-K levels as synthetic products such as Miracle Gro (24-8-16).

FERTILIZERS	NITROGEN	PHOSPHORUS	POTASSIUM
Alfalfa meal	2	5	1
Bone meal	3	15	0
Blood meal	13	0	0
Cottonseed meal	5	2	1
Fish meal	3	16	0
Rock phosphate	0	3	0
MANURES	NITROGEN	PHOSPHORUS	POTASSIUM
Guano	13	5	2
Poultry manure	4	3	1.9
Steer manure	2	0.54	1.9
Horse manure	0.7	0.3	0.5

Tips for applying mulch:

- Use what you have, or what's cheap or free.
- Wait to apply mulch until after plants have sprouted and soil is warm.
- Don't pile mulch up against the trunk or stem of any plant.
- Strive for at least 1 inch clear of mulch around the stem of the plant.

- Avoid tilling mulch in at the end of the season.

- Use mulch to keep walking areas clean and mud-free.

- Strive for a layer 2 inches thick for maximum benefit.

- Use mulch to protect new seedlings of fall crops from late summer heat.

- Water the ground thoroughly before adding mulch.

THE UNIVERSAL SOLUTION TO EVERYTHING

If all this soils talk has your head spinning, fear not because there are only two things that really matter to organic gardeners and their soils. Virtually all the problems, from stunted crops to standing water, are due to lack of sufficient organic matter or nutrient deficiency. Whenever challenges arise, add quality compost to the soil and be generous as this solves structural issues as well as mild nutrient deficiency. If plants aren't responding, then go to the next solution and add organic fertilizer, which treats nutrient deficiency specifically. Finally, make sure there's enough moisture to make the most out of both solutions, and your garden is guaranteed to show its pleasure with vigorous results.

Yellowing foliage is just one symptom of nutrient deficiency that can be treated with compost and fish emulsion or other liquid-based fertilizers.

Bale straw is the most affordable, widely available, and easy to transport mulch for vegetable gardens. Also, spreading straw over the walking paths will keep your shoes out of the mud when tending or harvesting the vegetables.

If exposed to rain, grass hay becomes unsuitable for livestock due to fungal molds, so it's often super-cheap or free at feed stores. Because it can't be sold as feed, it's not kept with other bales so you must ask for it.

Building soil is the most important aspect of organic gardening. Creating healthy soil and keeping it fertile is key to providing your plants with the raw materials to better recover from short-term heat and drought. Good soil ensures a healthy immune system and reduces the risk of pests and diseases. Bio-intensive earth contains amazing microbes that actually help plants become more resistant to wilt. Above all, soil is the container into which we pour water, and its qualities determine how much is used by our plants and how little is lost to evaporation. If there's one thing you get right in this whole process, let it be soil building, because when you grow in good ground, very little can go wrong.

CHAPTER 5

Water

When the well is dry, we learn the worth of water.
—BENJAMIN FRANKLIN

In 1984, after moving to the mountains, I learned the worth of water when living on a 400-foot-deep well that gave just 5 gallons a minute, which is the minimum for household use. Eighteen years living there instilled in me a sixth sense for water use. If I left a toilet running and went off to work, I'd come home to a dry well. This is an example of one driving force behind water conservation awareness: the fear of running out.

The second force is cost. If the submersible pump was damaged, then it would cost at least $1,000 to pull the pump for repair. If the pump was burned out, it was another thousand to replace it.

Today, I live in a desert community where the cost of county-supplied water is tiered. The first tier is metered at a lower cost for basic use, but when use exceeds that level, then the cost goes up. This increase is the penalty for going beyond what is considered standard household usage.

MICRO-SPRAY EMITTER

This emitter functions like a standard sprinkler head in low-pressure drip systems. It's set atop a pencil-like spike that moistens an area about 12 inches in diameter. Spray emitters won't wet the soil as deeply as standard emitters and may promote surface rooting.

SPAGHETTI TUBING

Lateral lines that feed emitters are ¼-inch diameter, which is so narrow it earned the nickname spaghetti tubing. These lateral lines branch off the supply line to bring individual emitters to individual plants.

This emitter is designed for use at the end of a spaghetti tube line to feed an individual plant.

These scenarios show the three driving forces that encourage us to use less water: shortage, cost, and penalties.

Irrigating in the most efficient way is key to growing annual plants in the desert, and in drought or dry times. Since the development of the drip system in the mid-twentieth century, there has been a revolution in how we grow crops. Rather than broadcast water over many square feet of ground using old-fashioned sprinklers, or run it wholesale down furrows, we now deliver water to each and every plant through its own personal emitter (a small, plastic, button-shaped fitting that's inserted into the supply line or placed at the end of lateral lines to deliver water to a specific location). It's small scale, intimate, and ideally suited to home vegetable gardens.

ISRAEL'S NECESSITY WAS THE MOTHER OF INVENTION

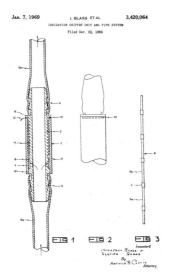

The actual patent drawing by Blass and his associates shows the original design of the drip emitter though it has evolved considerably since 1969.

A Polish-born Jewish engineer, Simcha Blass, working at the epicenter of Israeli hydrology, sought to help his people grow crops in the desert, where water is in extremely short supply. While Blass was the primary hydraulic engineer in Palestine, he spent much time in the desert, where many tales are told of his inspiration. One such tale finds him beneath a large fig tree eating lunch. A pipe nearby was perpetually dripping, and was the only sign of moisture to this tree. The engineer could not understand how such a large tree could survive with so little moisture, so he dug a hole to determine exactly how the drops of moisture could feed such a large plant. His discovery was a deep, onion-shaped wet zone underground that remained perennially moist because there was no surface evaporation. The fig had tailored its root system to feed off this single column of moisture in the ground, growing just as productive as other fig trees under flood irrigation.

This epiphany drove Blass to design a new kind of water-conservative irrigation that was affordable and easily manufactured using new plastics that solved problems of flow rates, friction loss, and pressure changes. By 1960, Blass had a prototype emitter about the size of a thimble that compensated for pressure, delivering water at a static rate.

The story goes that there was much skepticism, because agriculturists who were trained on the large, spreading-root-zone mentality simply did not trust such a solution. They could not think outside the box. Blass approached each kibbutz with his prototype but only Hatzerim kibbutz, a collective desert farm, was willing to give it a try. The new emitters were such a success that Blass patented his new products. In 1965 he established Netafim (Hebrew for "drops of water") Irrigation Company, giving the kibbutz 80 percent ownership and himself just 20 percent . Today Netafim (Netafim. com) is a worldwide presence wherever there is a need for solving problems of aridity and desertification.

Every drip irrigation system can be traced back to Simcha Blass and his pioneering work in Israel. Necessity became the foundation for many innovations in this unusual style of water delivery. His discoveries have transformed arid regions around the world, feeding millions where drought and famine have been historic.

WHAT IS A DRIP SYSTEM?

If you've never worked with a drip system before, it's important to get a conceptual view of what it entails. A drip system is more accurately called "low-pressure irrigation" because it operates at a water pressure level that is vastly reduced from standard plumbing. Low pressure means you can piece it all together by hand just like a giant Lego system without glue or rigid pipe. No special skills are required, but you need an idea of where you need water and how to get it there.

TIP: If you want to run a system off a faucet but need to keep it open for a garden hose, install a splitter. These handy little Y-shaped items are easy to find in the hose section of a hardware store. They screw onto the faucet, then split into two spigots, each with its own shut-off lever. The one that feeds the drip system stays open all the time while the one that feeds the hose is turned on and off with the lever.

There are two ways to create a drip system based on the water source: faucet and system. A faucet is drip system that is usually run off an outdoor faucet, which is why it's important to have a faucet close to your vegetable garden, and use a battery-operated timer to turn it on and off. A system is a drip system that also can be installed as part of your standard sprinkler system, so you can control it with the automatic sprinkler timer. This separate control is used because drip systems deliver water very slowly and in a different way than sprinkler systems, so a dedicated station in your controller allows you to set it to water at the exact times needed.

GPM/GPH

Irrigation heads used for lawns and flower beds have a rating in gallons per minute (GPM). A drip irrigation emitter delivers water so slowly that it's rated at gallons per hour (GPH).

PROBLEMS WITH LEAKY PIPE

Black hoses sold as "leaky pipe" or "soaker hose" are often confused with drip-system tubing, yet they are very different. Leaky pipe is composed of a porous material that water can move through when pressurized like a standard 60 PSI garden hose. The far end of each leaky pipe is capped off so once attached to the faucet, it fills up and pressurizes the water. This in turn forces water to seep out through the length of the hose. The problem is pressure. It's higher at the source, usually a faucet, then declines over the length of this hose. Therefore plants at the supply end will get more water than those at the far end. This problem was solved by the invention of the pressure-compensating drip emitter, which ensures every plant on a drip system receives the same amount of water.

PSI

Pounds per square inch (PSI) is the way water pressure at the faucet is rated. A common rating for residential water supply is 60 PSI. A drip system operates at 15 to 30 PSI. Static PSI in your neighborhood can drop in the morning when everyone is in the shower, which can sometimes affect traditional sprinkler system performance.

WITH HARD WATER, DON'T SET IT AND FORGET IT

In many areas, the water supply contains high amounts of soluble minerals, which create hard water. Two indicators of hard water are white mineral buildup on plumbing fixtures and lack of suds from soap. Drip systems under these conditions may accumulate minerals inside the tiny orifices of fittings and spaghetti tubing, which can interfere with flow rates or plug the fitting entirely. With hard water you can't just set it and forget it. You must check frequently to ensure every emitter is working properly. Failure of a single emitter during the dead heat of summer can kill a healthy plant in just a day or two. Be attentive to the first signs of wilt, which may be your clue that something is amiss.

This newly installed basic system shows how to pipe to each plant. It's easy to see the micro-spray heads, but this design is equally suited to drip emitters.

GET STARTED WITH A KIT

If you've never used a drip system before, the best way to start is with a kit that has the materials you need, including detailed instructions. A kit should include a filter, pressure reducer (a fitting that lowers the standard PSI of your water source—which would blow a low-pressure drip system apart the moment you turned it on), two sizes of piping, and emitters, plus other supplies necessary to set it up. This gives you hands-on experience with a system to make it more familiar,

The accumulation of minerals on this dripline shows exactly where the emitter orifice is located. Let too much efflorescence build up, and it may restrict the flow rate or clog this orifice entirely.

The smaller pressure reducer must be the first item in line followed by the filter, which is designed for a much lower operating pressure.

With emitters hidden under plants or mulch, it's important to check often for restrictions, which frequently result from hard-water mineral accumulations.

before you have to shop for bits and pieces. The best part about drip systems is that the supplies are cheap, so don't hesitate to buy more connectors, emitters, and tubing to allow the kit to better adapt to your garden's individual needs. Kits are available in the drip system section of the garden center, but these may be limited because they are created for the widest possible applications. Growing vegetables is very specific, so you'll want a kit that's best suited to your application.

DRIPWORKS KITS

The best kits can be found in the DripWorks catalog because these are more extensive than the one-size-fits-all kit at the garden center. They also offer more advanced Drip Tape Kits preferred by farmers who are growing in much longer rows than the standard raised bed. These are recommended for very large in-ground family gardens. The simple in-ground Garden Bed Irrigation Kits are available according to the size of your garden, so be sure to select one large enough to get the job done.

TIP: Drip system kits typically include a simple punch to make holes for emitters and fittings in ½-inch supply line. Many gardeners, particularly women who lack hand strength, find the standard hole punch difficult to use. It's advisable to invest $15 in a Miracle Punch that works just like a staple gun to make a crisp, accurately positioned hole with very little effort.

Deluxe: Waters up to eighteen 4-foot by 8-foot beds.

Standard: Waters up to nine 4-foot by 8-foot beds.

Economy: Waters up to three 4-foot by 8-foot beds.

Kits do not include timers that you program to turn the water on and off. This is the most important part of your system because it ensures a standard amount of water is delivered during a set time interval. Vegetable plants perform best under even and continuous moisture levels, so it's not dependent on you remembering to turn it on. The timer allows you to apply water in the best way for your soil. For example, sandy ground requires less water applied at more frequent intervals.

‖‖

BATTERY-OPERATED TIMER

The best investment you'll ever make is the purchase of an automatic timer for your drip system. This device turns it on and off on a schedule, as is done for a standard sprinkler system. Batteries eliminate the need for hard-wiring so you can install a timer anywhere. Timers typically run on a 9-volt battery, but some new models are solar powered. Most feature a digital LCD readout that takes the guesswork out of programming. The timer is installed between the faucet and the start of the supply line. Battery timers average about $50.

Note the size and visibility of the LCD readout because those with larger screens make it easier for an at-a-glance assessment. If your timer is exposed to direct sun, shelter it under a piece of cloth to extend the life of the LCD screen.

SUPPLY LINE

The standard supply line for a drip system is made of ½-inch diameter flexible tubing that brings water quickly to smaller lateral lines that feed emitters. You can add "in line" emitters directly to the ½-inch supply line to deliver more water to row crops.

EMITTER OPTIONS BY CROP

This guide shows how the size of a vegetable plant and its relative spacing dictates the type of emitters you'll need. Standard emitters are sized to deliver water at different rates. The lowest is just 1 GPH, while 4 GPH emitters suit larger needs. Mix and match these emitters according to the size and demands of individual plants. Over the years a variety of emitters have been created to suit specific situations for ornamental gardens and large-scale agriculture.

In the left bed, squash was planted adjacent to each of the inline drip emitter locations. It's essential to lay out the inline drip tubing first, turn it on to show exactly where emitters are in dry soil, and then plant your seed or seedling knowing exactly where the water is.

The spacing should match the individual crops you grow. Small, tightly spaced plants utilize ¼-inch dripline tubing. Larger row crops are best served by ½-inch tubing. Both the ½-inch and ¼-inch tubing is made with pressure-compensating emitters preinstalled at designated spacing. The ½-inch tubing has spacing from 9 to 36 inches between emitters. The ¼-inch tubing offers 6-, 9-, and 12-inch spacing.

Individual plants that are long-lived and demand a lot of water late in the season are best given their own separate emitters; a very large, prolific tomato may need more than one at peak season. This is important because undersized drip systems may not be able to provide enough water during a heat wave or in ultradry desert conditions.

¼-INCH DRIPLINE TUBING: beet, chard, carrot, lettuce, kale, kohlrabi, onion, radish, spinach, turnip

¼-INCH DRIPLINE TUBING: bean, broccoli, brussels sprouts, cabbage, cauliflower, collards, corn, cucumber, eggplant, okra, pea, pepper, potato, tomato

INDIVIDUAL EMITTERS: melon, pumpkin, squash (summer), squash (winter), tomato

CHANGE THE THINGS YOU CAN

To fine-tune your drip system over the season, you have two very effective ways to change the way water is applied. The equation of frequency and duration must balance properly for optimal water use by your plants.

Frequency

This dictates how often the system operates in 24 hours. When you first plant your garden, consider setting the timer for a twice-daily irrigation to keep the ground moist enough for seeds to germinate and so young seedlings don't dry out. As plants grow larger, they are less vulnerable, so you can switch back to once a day.

Duration

This is the length of time your system is turned on. The longer the duration, the more water applied. Duration is shorter early in the season when temperatures are cool and evapotranspiration rates are lower. As the season heats up, gradually increase the duration so water percolates deeper down, drawing roots to the cool moisture in the heat of the day. During late summer and into fall when cool-season crops begin and humidity is low, reduce duration and return to the twice-a-day frequency.

ADJUSTING YOUR DRIP SYSTEM

Vegetable-garden irrigation of any kind is always in a state of flux because your plants are too. Not only do their needs increase as they age, the temperatures rise through the season for double demand.

In the beginning, first-time drip system users will have some trial and error in determining how long and how often to run the system. The first days after planting require a lot of scrutiny because too little water will show in drooping leaf tips. It also can result in seed that fails to germinate. To get it right,

TIP: If you're a dry-times water conserver and rain does fall periodically during the summer, don't forget to turn off your drip system timer. If you get a heavy rain, leave it off for a couple of days, particularly in clay soil, because it will be thoroughly saturated.

TIP: Annuals are programmed to slow down with the shorter days, low humidity, and drying winds of autumn. Don't turn off the water on summer crops. Just be sure you adjust duration accordingly so they don't think the season is over and stop growing altogether. If you are growing a cool-season fall and winter garden, make sure those seedlings are not shorted the water they need to develop properly before temperatures drop precipitously. This demonstrates why some gardeners run two drip systems to fine-tune the often-overlapping transitions as warm-season crops slow and cool-season ones speed up.

start watering for just 5 minutes per day, then observe for a day or two. Increase watering time if you see any signs of stress. In sandy soils, you may choose to water twice a day (morning and evening) rather than increasing duration, since water moves through so quickly and evaporates just as fast on the surface.

The growing tips are where your plants talk to you in the language of wilt. Dehydration can begin with color changes followed by slight droop and finally true wilt. If the weather is unusually hot or windy, add a few minutes or split watering times. Just make sure to drop it down again after such conditions pass. Once you recognize these signs you'll be able to tell at a glance when longer duration is necessary. You may expect some wilt in the heat of the afternoon, but as long as the plants perk up after sunset, they will be fine.

One caution: the signs that tell you a plant is too dry are sometimes identical to those of one that is too wet. This is a frequent problem in heavy clay soils. The only way to tell the difference is to insert your finger deep into the soil around the emitters and test by feel if it's wet or not. When slow-draining soils become saturated, water displaces oxygen, which starts a process of fermentation or rot. This destroys the roots' ability to take up water, denying moisture to the tips, which will wilt and look like they're dry. If the plant doesn't perk up immediately after watering, it's best to dig around and find out why.

This tinkering is all part of ET consciousness, which guides you in making micro-changes to your drip system throughout the growing season.

AN OCCASIONAL DEEP DRINK

Even if you are irrigating with a drip system, sometimes it's very helpful to give your plants a more thorough soaking. This generous watering with the garden hose moistens all the soil, not just that onion-shaped wet zone produced by emitters. When you use a water wand with a diffuser at the end, turn the pressure down so it's applied much more slowly for a thorough soaking. Gradually saturate all the soil around your plants, or water the entire raised bed. This is helpful to maintaining overall fertility in regions without summer rainfall. In that fertile earth you built up with compost to boost microbial activity, the populations of important organisms will slow or become dormant in super-dry ground. Watering this way every few weeks during the heat of summer maintains the microbes. When it's done in the early morning or late evening you can water down the plants themselves in the process. This washing reduces dust accumulations and discourages tiny pests like spider mites, whiteflies, and aphids.

FILTER

The small diameter of drip system fittings make them vulnerable to clogging. A filter is standard with your system to catch particulate matter in the water before it enters the smaller-diameter fittings. You won't have to clean the filter often with city water, but if your water source is a rain barrel or pond, or if you have hard, mineral-rich water, it may require more frequent cleaning to maintain peak efficiency.

FLEXIBILITY: MOVE IT, STORE IT, PROTECT IT

Even if you don't like the looks of your drip system in the garden, having it lie on top of the soil is more convenient than burying the lines for a variety of reasons. If it is easily accessible, you can:

- Move it indoors for the winter in mountain zones or wherever freeze damage may occur.

- Store it for the summer in very hot, low-desert communities to prevent tubing and fittings from becoming brittle due to excessive UV exposure.

- Remove it during a dormant season where rodent damage is common in winter or summer.

- Put it away during the rainy season to prevent trip-and-fall risk.

- Easily set the whole system aside so you can use a tiller or turn soil by hand.

- Remove it all together if the garden is to lie fallow for a season or all year.

- Easily take it apart and redesign it to suit the new season's garden layout.

- Easily check all connectors for signs of leaking, breaking, wear, or weakness.

CONSERVATION BEGINS AT THE HOSE

The least recognized cause of unnecessary water waste is a leaking hose. Experts estimate that a single pinhole in a garden hose can waste up to 170 gallons a day. Follow these guidelines to make your hoses last long, resist kinks, and rarely leak.

ERASE COIL MEMORY ON DAY ONE. All too often, a garden hose is brought home and hooked up in its original coils created at the factory. This also occurs when bringing a hose out of winter storage. Pulling on a hose that's literally molded into its coils leads to kinks. Before using a new hose, find an open area in the sun to uncoil it, then let it heat up for awhile to soften the rubber and erase the "coil memory." Afterward, coil it in loops sized best for your space.

The point where two hoses connect is prone to slight leaking, which is easily solved with a fresh washer.

INVEST IN QUALITY. Not all hoses are the same. Cheap hoses are lightweight; quality hoses are expensive and heavy. Kinks in cheap hoses quickly turn into invisible cracks that waste water. If you think you can't afford to buy a quality hose, you'll end up buying two, and the second will inevitably be that expensive brand.

TURN IT OFF AT THE FAUCET. When using gun-like, hose-end nozzles, releasing your grip shuts off the water flow. It's easy to forget that the faucet is still on full blast, building up pressure inside the hose and stressing couplers. A forgotten hose can leak for days before you discover this, so make a point of turning the water off at the faucet and double-checking every time you use the hose.

NEVER TUG ON THE HOSE. Tugging is the biggest contributor of repeated kinking because there's so much pressure on the rubber and couplers and outdoor faucet piping. Tugging on older PVC faucets made fragile by exposure to UV and weathering can easily result in underground cracks that seep all the time, or a more obvious break.

KEEP AN EYE ON THE COUPLERS. The coupler at the faucet and those used to attach two hoses depend on washers to prevent leaking. When washers dry out or crack, seepage begins. Replace your washers every spring as part of early-season garden prep.

A dial timer allows you to manually turn on the system for a given amount of time, then the faucet turns off automatically. This method is a fail safe, so it's never left on and forgotten.

> **TIP:** Install a simple dial timer between the faucet and the hose. Use it every time you turn on the water so if you forget or are called away, or turn it off at the nozzle, there's a failsafe in place.

RAINWATER HARVESTING

Rainwater harvesting is simply capturing runoff to hold for future use. This requires a tank or cistern to contain your water supply until it's needed. If you're fortunate enough to have occasional summer rain, the ability to harvest it to use in your vegetable garden can make a huge difference not only in plant health, but in your household water consumption too.

In places like Southern California, rainwater harvesting is strictly a winter activity. In much of that

> **GRAVITY FLOW**
> The effects of gravity on how rapidly water flows downhill and how much pressure can build up in the process.

The easiest rain barrel is made from half a 50-gallon plastic drum, which in this photo features a decorative veneer. An open rain barrel like this requires you to draw water in buckets to carry to plants.

Rain barrels are fully enclosed to keep the contents from evaporating. A faucet allows you to attach a hose to more easily bring water to plants.

state, there may be no rainfall from May to November, offering no opportunity to replenish your rain barrel. In the mountains, on the coast, or in monsoon states, harvesting summer rain is a useful method of conserving water during the growing season. This process of capturing and holding rain for use in a vegetable garden can be as simple as setting up a rain barrel or as complex as a fully piped delivery system. Innovative sustainable desert farming folks have developed more advanced ways of harnessing the monsoon rains on larger properties, using channeling methods inherited from Native Americans who design gardens to benefit from maximized runoff.

Delivery

The biggest challenge to rainwater harvesting is getting it from the rain barrel to the plants in your vegetable garden. The old-fashioned way is with buckets. But if you design your garden and water system properly by elevating a rain barrel with a faucet at the bottom, a garden hose can be used to connect the barrel faucet to its destination. On a flat site the only pressure comes from the weight of the water in the barrel, but if there's the slightest rise in the length of the hose, gravity flow may not be enough. That's why elevating the barrel just a few inches can make this hose delivery foolproof. This demonstrates why it's so important to consider rainwater harvesting when selecting the place for your water-conserving vegetable garden.

OLLA

In the Southwest, Native American potters produced a water jar called an olla. This jar was designed to absorb some of the water it held, saturating the clay body of the pot. It was hung in the shade of a ramada or a tree, and the moisture evaporating through the pot cooled its contents even in extreme heat. Native American gardeners of desert regions discovered they could bury a small clay pot beside the roots of a plant and fill it. Gradually, moisture traveled through the clay to be available to the roots for extremely efficient watering. Today, some companies are producing these garden water ollas, which you can buy and plant next to a pepper or tomato to keep it moist in the height of summer. A less-expensive option is to puncture a plastic milk jug or liter soda bottle with fine needle holes, then bury it to its neck in the root zone. Fill periodically and adjust flow-through rate by screwing on the cap.

Homemade olla

CISTERNS

A cistern is simply a water tank buried underground. These are often used in the Southwest, where a great deal of rain falls during monsoon storms and residents need to store it for household or garden use, especially if their home is off the grid. The earth also insulates the container, typically thick plastic, from overheating or from UV exposure damage, which can shorten its life span. Burial also

A gallon of water weighs just over 8 pounds. Watering a vegetable garden by bucket carried from a cistern, well, or rain barrel gets old fast. For many, it's an impossible task. Watering plants close to the barrel is doable, but in reality, carrying a lot of water is difficult, so plan to reserve it for emergency water applications.

protects from freezing temperatures in colder climates. The problem with underground cisterns is that they have no potential for gravity flow delivery because they are set below grade. This reservoir requires an electric or gasoline-fired pump to draw up the water for use in irrigation or to pressurize water to move it a longer distance to a garden.

GRAY-WATER HARVESTING

Gray water is used household water recycled for other purposes. Not all household water is the same. This is why gray water got a bad reputation and many communities banned its use. The biggest problem with gray water is the presence of diseases such as E. coli, which can be problematic if the contaminated water is applied to vegetables. The widespread use of gray water or sewage water for irrigation can result in disease organisms on crops. In Mexico, the rule is to avoid any vegetable that isn't peeled before eating, expressly because of this bacteria problem. Gray water also can contain accumulations of soap or cleaning products that can build up when applied to the soil over long periods of time. Given these caveats, the potential for gray water augmenting your garden irrigation is still a very real solution.

TIP: How many times have you poured the remnants of a glass of water, a bottle of water, or other clean, unused excess water down the drain? If the least you do is harvest these from everyday use, you can make a difference. If your kids see this early in life, they'll take up your habit and make a difference too.

The most doable way to harvest gray water is to reuse water from your bathtub or washer. The clothes washer produces so much wastewater that folks in rural areas often pipe it outdoors so it doesn't fill up the septic tank. It's easy to remove the drain hose from the standpipe behind your washer, then use a hose clamp to add an extension to run outside through the floor or a wall. It may be difficult if your washer is in a tight location on a slab floor or where there are no adjacent outer walls.

To harvest this gray water, you need to avoid laundry products such as fabric softeners and soaps loaded with perfumes and other agents. In the average supermarket, the best detergent is Arm & Hammer Free, which contains no bleaches, perfumes, fabric softeners, or other additives. Where there is plentiful winter rain, accumulations of soapy residue from gray water are diluted and leached away. Where rainfall is minimal, this leaching won't take place and over time the residue will increase to toxic levels.

The rule of thumb when it comes to watering when there's little water to be had is to utilize harvested rainwater first, gray water second, and only use piped water for irrigation after the previous two sources are exhausted. Strive for progress and don't expect perfection because this process of applying water to plants may be the hardest thing for gardeners to learn and truly understand. Whole volumes have been written on the subject and the technology is changing every day. As water supply declines and population increases, the need for conservation will grow, whether a drought is on or not.

CHAPTER 6

Insects and Pests

Flying insects, dependent on plant life that has become
increasingly sterile, are flocking to residential areas—
backyards and public landscapes—in search of flowers,
plants and water.
—*THE DESERT SUN,* JULY 2014

In times of little rain and in environments plagued by drought, the availability of food for insects and other forms of wildlife becomes limited. This in turn drives them into our irrigated gardens in ever greater numbers. A little-known fact of the 1930s drought that caused the Dust Bowl is that swarms of grasshoppers swept over the land like a Biblical plague, consuming everything in their path. Whenever there are anomalies of weather, be it extremes of heat, cold, wind, or drought, certain insects proliferate and others may disappear altogether. The pests that matter to gardeners are those that threaten our vegetable plants.

There are volumes written on organic pest control and a technique called integrated pest management, so this chapter will focus on the basics of prevention, including some highly effective nontoxic controls.

Not all garden pests are insects. In drought, virtually all wildlife becomes stressed, so mammals, rodents, and reptiles may adopt new behaviors in order to survive. For example, water in our drip systems becomes highly attractive to ants that invade emitters. Ground squirrels and wood rats chew through plastic tubing. Even if you've never had pest problems in the past, all bets are off in drought years. The moisture in the leaves of vegetables such as bean plants or Swiss chard becomes highly attractive to sucking insects that flock to them in droves.

Even underground, there's the risk of gophers and chipmunks tunneling far and wide seeking the few still living roots that aren't dried to a crisp.

PREVENTION IS THE BEST MEDICINE

Plants have an immune system against pests and diseases, but like humans, when they are stressed by drought, their immunities decline. Botanists know that if pests strike a group of plants, they tend to attack the weakest individual first. There they build up numbers before moving on to the healthier ones. This is why

The praying mantis is a valuable beneficial insect and ferocious predator that keeps undesirable pests under control.

growing vegetables in a hot, dry desert or elsewhere under minimal moisture requires perpetual vigilance. Problems—caught early—can be easily controlled, but infestations can be fatal.

Secondly the pressure of plant-hungry wildlife forces you to be attentive to protecting your garden physically. Under drought stress, animals will eat plants they wouldn't touch in a normal year. This is why deer-resistant plant lists are so iffy. These browsers can change preferences significantly when they are abnormally hungry. In the desert, rabbits avoid eating cactus, but when the rain doesn't fall as it should, they will brave the spines to access this moisture-rich succulent plant.

ABOVE ALL, PROTECT THE BENEFICIALS

Essential to organic gardening is understanding the relationship of predator and prey in the insect world. Prey species are plant-eating pests. Predators, called "beneficial insects," exist to keep populations of prey species under control. The reason pesticides are not used in the organic garden is because they are broad-spectrum killers that destroy both predator and prey. Since prey

TIP: If you live in the desert, predator insects may not survive extreme heat over the summer, so plan to import a new crop each fall to maintain a sufficient population.

species are more numerous in general, they inevitably reinvade later, after the pesticide has dissipated. Predator insects are much slower to return. Without predator species in place to control them, plant eaters proliferate rapidly into much larger populations than normal. That's what causes infestations.

INSECT PREDATORS: ladybugs, praying mantis, lacewing, hover fly, parasitic wasps, spiders

ANIMAL PREDATORS: lizards, frogs, snakes, rats, birds, owls, hawks

Lizards make superior dry garden residents because they feed on all sorts of pests.

INCREASE YOUR PREDATOR POPULATION

The best way to protect your organic garden is to boost the natural populations of beneficial insects. You can buy living bugs or egg cases to release directly into your garden, concentrating them where needed the most. Some predators attack certain kinds of prey, while others are more general in their preferences. For example, releasing ladybugs helps to control aphids. Introducing preying mantis egg cases to your organic garden in spring can make a big difference in pest populations over the coming growing season because they feed on so many different pests.

Predator bugs are now sold at most garden centers and home improvement stores, but online catalogs are the best way to obtain the less common types. Bugs tend to be on sale in spring and summer during the growing season, but in warmer, low-desert regions the growing

You can buy dormant egg cases for praying mantises, which you place in the garden where they'll hatch out tiny versions of the adult insect called nymphs.

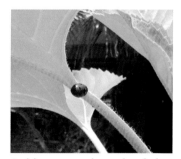

Ladybugs are predators that feed on tiny insects such as aphids.

season begins in October, when "good bugs" may not be in stores. Consider ordering from Arbico and other catalogs listed in the Resource (page 197) of this book to find sources that ship good bugs throughout the year.

DOMESTIC CATS

Although house cats hunt rodents, they also kill lizards and birds, two of our most effective forms of natural pest control.

Domestic cats are quintessential predators that keep rodent populations under control in home, garden, and barn. However, their activities can be devastating in the organic garden. While all cats are not equally relentless hunters, it's their nature to kill lizards and other forms of wildlife that are vital to the predator-prey balance. Small reptiles and ground-nesting birds like quail can be crucial to keeping insects under control, particularly in rural areas, and if cats are allowed to prowl the home site they may deplete these important populations. Once predator populations have been decimated, large infestations of insects normally consumed by these smaller reptiles quickly follow.

Using insect weight row covers early in the season is an ideal method for protecting seedlings from pests naturally.

DAILY OBSERVATION IS KEY TO PREVENTION

The key to pest control in your water-efficient garden is daily observation of the plants and how they're faring. Try to observe each and every plant to get a clear idea of how they look when all systems are go. That way if something is amiss, you'll recognize it immediately. When you catch pest problems early, they are easy to fix and don't have lasting consequences, but if the problem persists over time, it can lead to a serious infestation.

LET THE DRIP SYSTEM GUIDE YOU

Most gardeners check their plants while hand-watering, but when growing with drip systems on a timer, we need not be there for watering to occur. That makes it easy to lose touch with the plants. If you're a beginner, the best way to get started with daily observation is to check every emitter on the system each day. This often requires you to get down to soil level to see the emitters, which is close enough to spot even the smallest insect pests. It's not uncommon, by the way, for poorly seated emitters or connectors to pop out of the tubing. Not only does it leave the plant it's feeding flooded, but a lost emitter alters the static pressure, which reduces flows to the emitters and may short plants of water at the end of the line. If you're tending to your drip irrigation properly, you'll catch the first signs of pests in the process.

TIP: Row covers used to protect crops from cold can also be a big benefit for your seedlings. These tunnel-shaped enclosures help keep seedlings from exposure to pests early in the season so they will be off to a good, clean start. You can also lay the row cover fabric directly on the plants because it's so lightweight. Be sure to remove the row covers when plants start to flower, so pollinators can reach them.

FIVE STEPS TO LEAST TOXIC PEST CONTROL

When new gardeners find pests, the tendency is to douse them with pesticides. However, with organic gardens, we start with the least toxic method of pest control and then ramp up incrementally until control is achieved. First, accurately identify the invaders, then follow these steps:

Large bugs are easily handpicked from the plants to reduce their numbers to more manageable levels.

1. **PICK 'EM OFF:** Handpicking is the best way to remove larger bugs that are easy to see. Caterpillars of every kind are removed this way, as are some beetles. Ditto grasshoppers. Wear gloves if they gross you out! Be careful when disposing of them so they don't reinvade the garden.

2. **HOSE 'EM OFF:** Smaller pests such as aphids tend to cluster on the new growing tips of a plant. Shoot the tip with a strong jet of water and you can knock them back significantly. Whiteflies dwell on the back of the leaves, and it requires more attention to get water under there. Washing your plants occasionally is a good idea because it removes insect eggs and washes away dust accumulations where spider mites proliferate. However, never wash your plants in direct sun because water drops act like a magnifying glass and can burn leaf tissues. The best time is in early morning so water dries quickly before sun hits it, and before fungal diseases benefit from the moisture. During drought, folks growing with a drip system may never think to hose down the plants because that demands more water. Don't let this discourage you, because it's very important. To conserve, use a nozzle that gives you a strong jet without delivering much volume.

3. **APPLY NONTOXIC CONTROLS:** Soap is known to be toxic to many insects. Organic gardeners mix their own homemade insecticidal soap to spray on their edibles, or buy it ready mixed to save time. To make your own, use non-detergent liquid soap such as Ivory or Dawn. Mix at a ratio of 1 tablespoon of soap per quart of water, then pour into a spray bottle, or a pump sprayer for larger gardens. When picking and hosing aren't enough, apply insecticidal soap to kill the remaining pests. Plan follow-up applications weekly to catch any bugs that survived.

4. **APPLY BIOCONTROLS:** Biocontrols are products that harness the natural substances or organisms to kill insects. There are different biocontrols for certain bugs, so this isn't a broad-spectrum approach. Because caterpillars are among the most damaging of all plant eaters, they have been traditionally difficult to control even with chemical pesticides. The most effective control is called Bt, which harnesses living bacteria, *Bacillus thuringiensis*, in an easy-to-apply solution. Bt is nontoxic to humans yet highly successful on caterpillars and the dreaded tomato hornworm. Another organism, milky spore disease, is sold as a biocontrol of

Japanese beetles. Biocontrols are the most promising forms of pest management in organic food crops.

5. APPLY BOTANICAL PESTICIDES: When all else fails, resort to botanical pesticides. Certain plants contain natural chemicals that repel and even kill insects. The pyrethrum daisy, *Tanacetum coccineum* is the source of pyrethrins, the most widely used botanical pesticide. Do be aware that pyrethrins are a broad-spectrum killer that impacts beneficial insects as well. Neem is another common example of a botanical pesticide. It originates in the seed of a tropical tree from India and is extracted for use in home gardens.

UNHOLY TRINITY: APHIDS, SCALE, AND ANTS

Although ants don't damage plants per se, keep a sharp eye out for them as indicators that something else is going on. This is because ants love to consume honeydew, the residue of aphids and scale insects, which is usually clear or green.

In scenarios where a lot of honeydew accumulates, black mildew-like fungus takes up residence on the surface. Ants so love honeydew they actually help aphids and scale infest your plants just like ranchers spread their cattle around to "greener pastures." The moment you see ants in the garden, promptly wash down the plants to remove any pests feeding the ants, then keep a sharp eye out for their return. Traps also help guard against ants reestablishing their ranches among your veggies.

Many kinds of tiny caterpillar pests announce their presence with tiny holes like these in collard greens.

HORRIBLE HORNWORMS AND OTHER PROBLEM CATERPILLARS

A single mature hornworm can eat all the flowers off your tomato plant in just one night. They'll spread to your peppers and eggplants too. Hornworms are larvae of moths that live to eat. Virtually all other caterpillars are threats to your plants too, because they can ruin them so quickly. The first sign of their presence is missing leaves and flowers or small, rounded, BB-like excrement on leaves. Caterpillars know how to hide in the foliage and have always been a challenge to farmers because no chemical pesticide was very effective. Then Bt hit the market and control became simple and nontoxic. When you see any sign that caterpillars are at work, apply Bt right away because the pests must consume leaves that have this organism on them. Because moths lay their eggs in clusters, where there's one hornworm there are probably dozens more in hiding, and the potential for damage increases exponentially every day.

A single mature hornworm can consume whole sections of tomato plants almost overnight.

Consuming tomato leaves with Bt kills the hornworm and most other caterpillar species.

Even if you don't see any caterpillars, these pellet-like feces tell you they're in there and it's time for Bt.

BIRDS

Birds in the vegetable garden are helpful in terms of consuming unwanted insect pests, but in drought or dry times they can be problematic too. The old association of crows in cornfields is one example of unwanted feeding behavior. Damage to tree fruits is another.

Desert gardeners have long known that extreme dry conditions can lead birds to feed on plants due to their moisture content. They'll do the same in drought regions as well. The lack of green vegetation lures birds to oasis-like vegetable gardens, where they'll peck ripening tomatoes. In drought, birds become omnivorous, digging up moist seedlings and eating flowers before fruits can form.

One way to keep birds out of the desert garden is to erect a framework for aviary netting to cover a small garden. For larger gardens, the best solution is to use insect-weight row covers.

The desert gardener's solution to bird predation is to erect a lightweight pole structure in the garden. It's then covered with plastic fruit tree bird netting or large-scale woven netting used in the horticultural trades. Plastic netting won't hold up very long, maybe 1 to 2 years. Woven netting holds up for years in the desert. It can be purchased in enormous pieces and cut to order. The netting keeps birds out but allows plenty of sun and pollinators in.

RODENT TUNNELS IMPACT WATER CONSERVATION

The desert may appear empty, but it's alive with many kinds of rodents that love to eat your plants. They spend the day in cool underground burrows, then come out at night to feed voraciously on anything they can find. Pack rats, chipmunks, ground squirrels, gophers, moles, voles, and rabbits are the most prevalent. Because these are digging pests, the biggest problem is their tunneling under fences and into your garden.

It's important to stay on top of populations because, even if they're not root eaters, their tunnels can interfere with the way water travels underground. Without surface evidence,

> **TIP:** Avoid using bait to kill rodents, particularly in rural areas. When these poisons kill a rodent, it becomes food for scavengers such as bobcats and coyotes, not to mention dogs and cats. By the time that animal has consumed enough to kill it, there's a significant concentration that can make a scavenger sick or die if it ingests the carcass.

burrows can exist deeper down where they act like a French drain to draw water out of the surrounding soil. Moisture in the soil is drawn away by the dry cavity of a tunnel. This can create surface soil evaporation conditions deeper down. Tunnels become a big source of waste when you water with the garden hose too, because water moves directly down into the tunnel and then runs far beyond the garden.

If large populations of rodents are allowed to accumulate, an immense warren of tunnels can cause even bigger problems. There is an important relationship between water conservation and rodent control, and, as with insects, it's always easier to solve a problem at the outset than to face a much larger infestation later on.

Hardware cloth tubes can be used to protect tomato plant stems from gnawing rabbits and other surface-feeding rodents.

These PVC wire mesh frames protect chard, kale, and other greens from rabbit damage.

THREE DEGREES OF SEPARATION: FENCING UNDERGROUND

Fencing out rodents might seem easy, but they will tunnel under the fence to enter the garden. Therefore you must create an underground fence to keep them out permanently. When creating underground barriers, bend a strip of fencing in half lengthwise and make your trench wide enough to accommodate the L-shaped piece outside the garden. That way, if a rodent encounters the fence and tries to tunnel down and under, it will only go down a few inches before encountering the horizontal barrier.

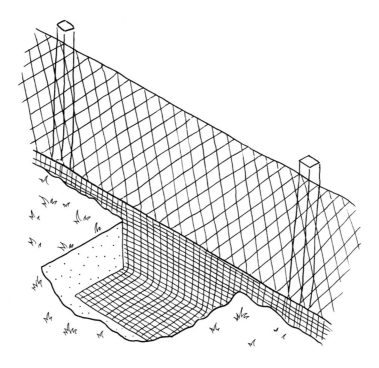

When creating underground barriers, bend a strip of fencing in half lengthwise and make your trench wide enough to accommodate the L-shaped piece outside the garden.

Other possible barriers:

SHEET METAL: Dig a trench along the base of your fence and line it with a strip of corrugated metal roofing. Buy new sheets or recycle them from discarded metal sheds that have been destroyed by weather or wind.

HARDWARE CLOTH: Dig a trench along the base of your fence and line it with small mesh hardware cloth. Recycled fine wire fencing also works.

Rabbits can destroy a whole garden of seedlings over night, so fencing the garden is essential to keep them, kids, and family pets out of the veggies.

NARCISSUS: All daffodil spring bulbs are toxic. Rodents won't touch them and prefer not to tunnel under them either. Save money by buying them in a large mix for naturalizing. Line them up around the edges of your garden. They are highly drought-resistant and grow without irrigation in most areas since they become dormant in the summer.

Straw bales are very wide, which discourages pests from tunneling under or through them. They also offer additional protection to short plants or seedlings by acting as a windbreak that stops blowing sand, so it won't tatter the tender new leaves.

STRAW BALES: An affordable way to create a barrier is to use straw bales set on edge. They are wide enough to discourage tunneling because rodents can't see or smell the plants on the other side. This is a good solution for the short-term, first-year garden. When the bales finally rot, carve out the center into a trench, fill with potting soil and grow your greens there. When that's no longer possible, they make excellent mulch. Bales also can be used to stabilize support poles for a net or shade-cloth covering to keep your vegetables pest free for the season.

TIP: In the desert, rodents will go to great lengths to drink water. Locals discovered a way to control pack rats without poison. Simply fill a 5-gallon plastic bucket with a foot of water. Rats will climb inside to drink and can't get out again, so they drown. This method is well proven and the carcass is suitable for scavengers. This desert trick also may be effective elsewhere during drought and in dry times.

LIVE TRAPS

Gardeners have been tasked with killing rats, gophers, and moles for eons. Though you may not like the idea of traps, they may be all that separates your garden from being decimated by hungry rodents. Trapping gophers is not easy and takes time to learn. For other rodents, live traps mean you can catch and relocate the rodent rather than kill it. Live traps that open only on one end are recommended, because the animal must go to the far end to obtain the bait.

TOP PEST AND ORGANIC SOLUTIONS

PEST	PRACTICAL	BIOCONTROLS	PESTICIDE	SIGNS
Aphids	Wash plants	Ladybugs	Insecticidal soap	Visible on the growing tips of plants and often associated with presence of ants
Cabbage worm	N/A	Parasitic nematodes	Bt	Circular holes followed by larger chewing of leaf and stem or small pelleted excrement
Potato beetle	Straw mulch	*Beauveria bassiana*	Neem	Holes in foliage that increase with warmer weather
Spider mites	Wash plants	N/A	Insecticidal soap	Silvering of top of leaf while pests feed on under-side; mites visible amid webby residue
Tomato hornworm	Handpick	N/A	Bt	Sudden and significant loss of flowers and growing tips followed by rapid defoliation
Whiteflies	Wash plants	N/A	Sticky traps	Silvering of leaf surface as pests congregate underneath; leaf movement causes them to fly

Birds keep your garden bugs under control, but in the desert where there's little food, they'll peck and eat ripening tomatoes and other crops.

Garden pest control is a broad and diverse subject that could fill volumes. What you must remember during drought and dry times is that healthy and fully hydrated plants will naturally resist insect damage. Equally important is keen daily observation to spot pests the moment they appear so that simple discouragement or organic or biocontrol products are effective. Failure to notice a growing population inevitably results in infestation. When numbers reach critical levels they threaten your whole crop. Think prevention through plant care, observation to spot the problem early, and control using the least toxic system.

Part 2
PRACTICE

In many ways, practice is what connects every gardener to the global community of plant growers. All must follow the same processes to grow food no matter where they dwell, with some deviations to account for climate and season. That's why it's so important to know how to choose the right plants for a droughty or desert garden. It's also about nurturing plants to maturity and tending them to harvest, which is no small thing when you're dealing with hot, dry winds and rationed water. Thankfully contemporary organic farmers have brought many excellent techniques into the marketplace to share with the residential gardener. Just a few years ago you couldn't find organic pesticides, row covers, or heirloom seed catalogs. Thanks to the demands of organic growers, today they are everywhere.

CHAPTER 7

Selecting Desert-Hardy Vegetables

*It is not the strongest of the species that survives, nor the
most intelligent that survives. It is the one that is most
adaptable to change.*
—CHARLES DARWIN

The Earth's climate is always in a perpetual state of change. We are either cooling
on our way toward another ice age or warming up from a previous one. On a
smaller scale, farmers know that every year will be slightly different depending
on the constellations of rain and temperature. With so much change going on,
plants must be equipped with genes that allow them to change with the Earth's
climate. From this large gene pool came many characteristics that define the contemporary garden vegetables we know today.

For centuries, farmers and plant breeders have been selecting seed of individual
plants that improves the quality of their crops. The chosen plants may have larger
fruits, greater yields, improved disease resis-
tance, a different growth habit, or enhanced
flavor. The places where these changes
took place tell us much about what the
farmer was seeking to better cope with local
environmental conditions.

LANDRACE

Vegetable varieties developed by
farmers and gardeners around
the world that are super-adapted
to the local microclimate. If that
farmer ceases to replant his landrace, it will vanish from existence
when the last viable seed dies.

HOW VEGETABLE VARIETIES DIFFER

Just because a plant is an heirloom doesn't make it better. In fact, planting the wrong heirloom can be a total disaster when it's not adapted to your garden or climate. To understand how the world of heirloom plants works, let's look at tomatoes as an example. This New World vegetable was native to Central and South America and therefore genetically equipped to perform well in hot climates. When it was grown in northern Europe or Britain, the cool summer, rainfall, and shorter growing season didn't allow enough time for the fruits to fully ripen. In the farms of this region, landraces evolved that fruited earlier under cooler conditions. Some of these evolved into named varieties with better adaption to summer rain, humidity, lower temperatures, and short seasons. These heirlooms will not grow well in the desert, or in drought or dry times because they are not adapted to growing in arid conditions and may actually demand more water than standard commercial varieties, particularly in hot climates.

HEIRLOOM

A term of affection for an old cultivar or landrace still in cultivation and thus available to buy from seed. The trend toward growing heirlooms helps keep varieties in continuous cultivation, which is the only way to preserve that plant's unique genetic characteristics for posterity.

Similarly, the original tomato evolved elsewhere in the Old World too. Farmers in northern Africa, the Middle East, and Persia had droughty conditions and extreme heat. In these regions, the farmers selected the most vigorous plants to create their landraces, and these produce some of the most desert-hardy plants possible. These heirlooms may not crack in high UV sunlight. They may be genetically programmed for growing with less water and their leaves may be smaller to lose less moisture in extreme low humidity and wind.

A study of American collard strains developed by small farms in various parts of the South revealed considerable visual differences within this species, each perfectly adapted to the microclimate of origin.

GMO: GENETICALLY MODIFIED ORGANISM

Scientists have learned how to solve problems by altering the genetic makeup of a plant. This ability is vital for coping with climate change when the food supply is threatened, by quickly creating a variety of food plants that is genetically resistant to the problem pest, disease, or climatic anomaly.

Unfortunately this technology has been exploited for profit and has become an unexpected threat to pollinators and other wildlife. For this reason, many gardeners have become aware of GMO vegetable seed as being a threat to the food supply by damaging pollinators and creating health threats to those who consume them. There's no question such new science is daunting and potentially dangerous. However, with the increasing threat of organisms invading whole new hemispheres, we can better understand how quickly a threat from plant viruses

Heirloom varieties of vegetable seed were developed before genetic engineering.

infecting wheat or corn can influence the food supply. Without the decades and centuries it takes to create landraces and test hybrids, GMOs may one day prove invaluable to combating devastating plant pests and diseases in a time frame short enough to compensate for the potentially staggering short-term losses.

PICKING VARIETIES FOR DESERT, DROUGHT, AND DRY TIMES

There are many characteristics unique to each vegetable variety, both modern and heirloom. It's important to know what to look for when selecting them for low-water gardens and for the rigors of desert climates. All of the varieties listed here are

SEED BANK

A place where seed with long-term viability can be preserved. Seed banks help to preserve genetic diversity that may prove the salvation of the food supply as climates change.

tailored to microclimates that experience difficult, arid conditions and periodic extreme drought.

KNOW YOUR GEOGRAPHY

Vegetable varieties are defined by their region of origin. Some varieties are developments by science for nations to improve food production and reduce famine. Knowing the names of these countries of origin or regions where breeders hoped to improve agriculture helps you zero in on a variety strictly by its designated climate preference.

Selecting vegetables that originate in climates around the world similar to yours will be your first requirement for success. These plants are also ideal for foodies who delve into the unique dishes of distant lands where their endemic varieties lend a particular character to their flavors. For example, Middle Eastern cuisine uses less-sweet tomatoes, and unless you grow them, your dishes may not be quite the same. This is something important to immigrants, and second generations who are trying to preserve their heritage may seek out such plants to assist in maintaining this culinary inheritance.

Look for varieties from two regions: extremely arid or moderately arid. If you are simply trying to minimize water use to help support the environment, select from both groups equally.

VIABILITY

The length of time a seed remains "alive" to grow into a plant. A short-term viability example is certain lettuce that loses viability after just one year. The record for extended viability is date seed from ruins thousands of years old that successfully germinated.

Extremely Arid Regions

Varieties from these regions should be a priority for desert gardeners. These zones around the world are home to vast deserts and very long dry seasons. They have often been the sites of famine, both throughout history and in the contemporary world. Vegetables developed here will be the best adapted to both high- and low-desert conditions, with very low humidity and significant wind. In this area, drought is always normal, so agriculture there will feature many of the rare and adaptable desert-born innovations.

NORTHERN AFRICA: Algeria, Egypt, Libya, Morocco, Sudan, Tunisia

MIDDLE EAST: Cyprus, Egypt, Iran, Iraq, Israel, Lebanon, Saudi Arabia, Syria, Yemen

ASIA MINOR: Armenia, Greece, Turkey

AMERICAN SOUTHWEST: Arizona, Colorado, Nevada, New Mexico, Texas, Utah

NORTHERN MEXICO: Chihuahua, Coahuila, Durango, Sinaloa, Sonora

CENTRAL AUSTRALIA: western Australia, Northern Territory, south Australia

Moderately Arid Regions

People who are growing during drought will find more diversity in varieties from these regions. Moderately arid locations experience a rainier winter than true desert, and in normal years the summer dry season may extend for six months or more without rain. When drought strikes in these "Mediterranean" climates, it causes a much greater impact due to vastly higher population and lack of alternative water sources.

MEDITERRANEAN: Cyprus, Eastern Europe, Italy, Portugal, Southern France, Spain

SOUTHERN AFRICA: Namibia, South Africa, Tanzania, Zambia, Zimbabwe

NORTH AMERICA: California

MESOAMERICA: Costa Rica, Guatemala, Honduras, Nicaragua, Panama

SOUTH AMERICA: Argentina, Chile, Peru

COASTAL AUSTRALIA: Perth, Adelaide

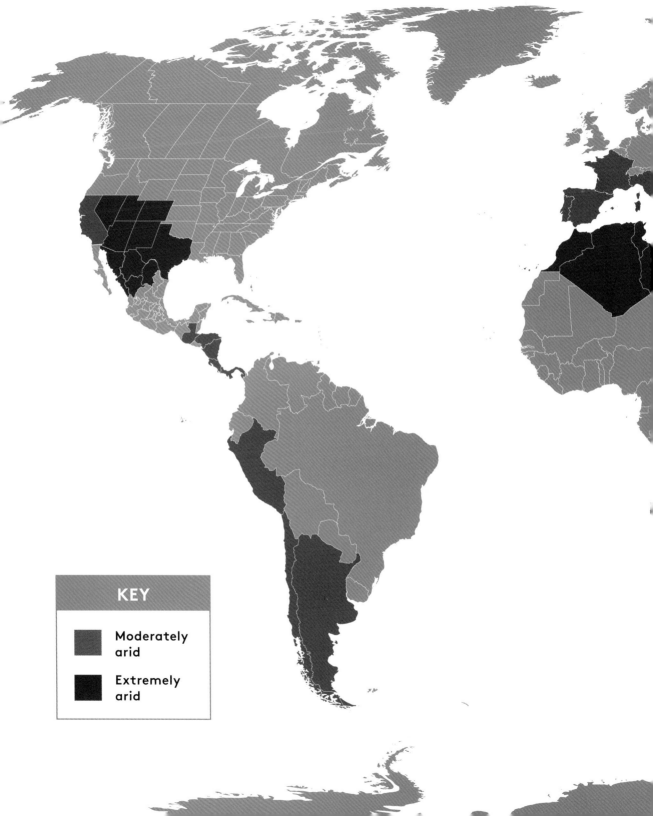

KEY

Moderately arid

Extremely arid

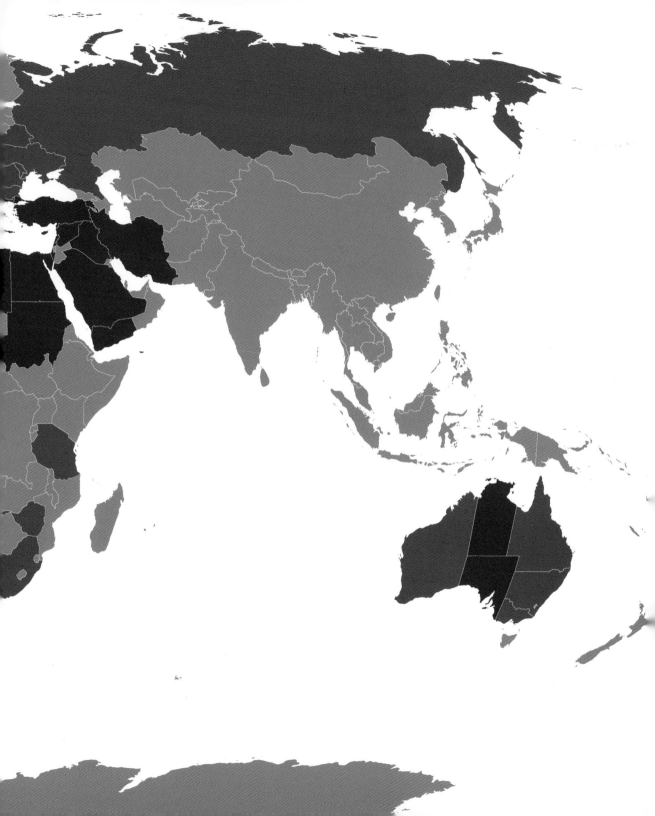

EXCEPTIONAL SEED SOURCES

Seed Savers Exchange

This communal global marketplace is actually two organizations, a non-profit and its catalog. Its original incarnation as a non-profit began in 1975 to connect gardeners and farmers around the world to share their heirloom and landrace seed with the membership. Think of it as a village marketplace where all the local farmers sold their unique landraces to newcomer farmers who wanted a better plant for their climate. Essentially, this is the only global seed marketplace where everyone can join to buy or sell with anyone else around the world. This "club" remains just as active today and is more accessible with the advent of the Internet. Now, instead of a printed catalog the size of a telephone book and placing orders through the US mail or international mail, you can browse and pay online and there's only one shipment, from the farmer to you. You can browse thousands of listings from around the world, many with digital images, a feature lacking in the original catalog. However, if you want to buy seeds, you must join this massive grassroots seed-trading organization first. There is no better gold mine for desert and drought gardeners because you get access to regional landraces directly from arid climates around the world. This is where knowing your geography really comes in handy! To browse these amazing listings, log on to exchange.seedsavers.org.

> **HYBRID**
>
> The result of two species that cross-pollinate naturally or are crossbred artificially by plant breeders. The seed produced from this cross will carry some genetic characteristics of either parent, with highly variable results. Seed of hybrid plants can be sterile.

> **TIP:** Many of today's seed houses offer their entire catalog to download from their websites. These large files allow you to instantly see the catalog on your phone, tablet, or computer without a lot of data transfer that can happen when shopping online. Digital catalogs also make it easier to search by keyword rather than using an index to find that special variety.

SSE Catalog: The Best of the Exchange

Over time, the Exchange realized that many people wanted to buy their plants but didn't want the hassle of making purchases from many different sources. This resulted in a new branch of the organization that obtained land to grow out the seed of the favorite Exchange discoveries. This created enough quantity to sell them in a traditional print and online catalog. See it at SeedSavers.org or order a catalog from (563) 382-5990.

MEMBER LISTINGS FROM SEED SAVERS EXCHANGE

Here are three very different examples of the way private members of the Exchange describe the seed they grow and are offering to the group.

MEXICAN GIANT

75 days, Beefsteak, 1–2 pounds, 4–5 inches in diameter. Pink tomato. Great slicer. Ind., reg. leaf. Outperformed many other beefsteaks in our desert clime. Reportedly a rare variety from Mexico.

MAKO AKOKOSRADE

Capsicum chinense. Plants produce abundant quantities of pointed, wrinkled, dark yellow peppers. By far, the most aromatic pepper variety I've encountered anywhere, with an intense habanero aroma, with strong notes of melon and even a little mango. Ghanaians use this to add extra aroma to peppery dishes. "Mako akokosrade" means "yellow pepper" in the Twi language. The original seeds were collected on 2011.08.29, at a roadside market in Nkrakum village, outside Koforidua, East Akyim District, Eastern Region, Ghana.

CORCHORUS OLITORIUS

Egyptian Spinach (Corchorus olitorius) aka Molokhia, Jute Leaf, and Jew's Mallow. This super-green has been widely eaten since the time of the pharaohs in the Middle East.

It was the "food of kings" packed with vitamins, minerals, and antioxidants. Grow this as an annual. Direct sow about ¼ inch deep May–July. These very tiny seeds are a weird green color so don't be surprised. I space these as close as an inch and grow straight upright stalks, but they would prefer 12 inches between them and to be pinched back to promote branching. These plants love lots of water, sun, heat, and humidity and grow about 5 feet tall if not pruned. The leaves can be harvested any time once established (about 120 days from planting). They transplant well. Leaves are edible both raw and cooked. We enjoy them as a textured addition to our summer salads. These greens also dry well to be used later to thicken stews or soup or to make tea. Egyptian Spinach is frost sensitive. Molokhia is a type of soup made from Egyptian Spinach. Many recipes are available online.

Baker Creek Heirloom Seed Co.

This may be the newest seed source in its group and among the best, dominating the market in recent years. What makes this supplier so useful is the extensive write-up given to each variety. This gives us details on exactly where a variety comes from and more extensive descriptions of its unique characteristics. Not all heirloom seed sellers go to such lengths to provide the data that helps us make choices of new strains that would extend our ability to cultivate food in a desert summer. It's well worth the cost to order their extensive color book, The Whole Seed Catalog ($7.95 in 2014) and the magazine Heirloom Gardener ($15.00/year). Among the articles of interest to desert gardeners in a recent Whole Seed Catalog were "Seeds To Afghanistan" and "Saving Syria's Seeds," which offered excellent reading on the origins and cultivation of vegetables in the Middle Eastern deserts. The annual Good Seeds Catalog is a smaller and more user-friendly free version of The Whole Seed Catalog. Get it free by requesting it at RareSeeds.com, where you can also shop online, or call (417) 924-8917.

Both RareSeeds.com and the Rare Seeds catalog are from Baker Creek.

CHIHUAHUA LANDRACE—BAKER CREEK HEIRLOOM SEEDS

We collected this squash from a roadside stand in the Mexican desert a little west of the city of Chihuahua. They vary a lot in color, all shades of green, white, yellow and possibly a few other colors. Fruit are large and attractive; used extensively in northern Mexican cuisine.

ABU RAWAN TOMATO—BAKER CREEK HEIRLOOM SEEDS

A variety contributed by our friend, expatriate Iraqi seed collector Nael Aziz. He stated that it is a bit unusual for an Iraqi type, because in Iraq the people tend to favor tart tomatoes, while this one is sweeter. Having solid, all-purpose flesh, it will take the heat, like Iraqi types generally. Named for the onetime caretaker of the greenhouses at the Agricultural College at Al Graib. Maintained in cultivation in private gardens there since the 1970s. In my desert garden, Abu Rawan produced perfect fruits, free of cracking, a common problem in extreme heat.

Native Seeds/SEARCH

Decades ago, when talk of an heirloom meant your grandmother's locket, a little-known organization was growing in the desert of Tucson, Arizona. Native Americans were suffering health problems and diabetes caused by a modern diet. Renowned botanists Gary Nabhan and Mahina Drees devoted their considerable knowledge and skill to helping the Tohono O'odham tribe improve their diets by rekindling their age-old agricultural practices. The tribal elders wanted to grow the same food crops as their ancestors did in the desert to carry on that heritage. This inspired the creation of one of the first heirloom seed houses, this one dedicated to preserving the micro-adapted strains of vegetables unique to a

Native Seeds/SEARCH encourages seed saving with helpful how-to articles and supplies on their website.

A number of indigenous corn strains from Native Seeds/SEARCH harvested from my garden.

specific climate. In this case, the rare plants were selected over many centuries to tolerate the poor soils, dry wind, and extreme heat under minimal water supply. Over time Nabhan and friends traveled far and wide to find isolated communities in the desert Southwest and rural northern Mexico where ancestral crops were still grown. Their efforts to not only rediscover these varieties, but to bring these crops back to Arizona and grow them in quantity literally revolutionized Native American agriculture. In times of drought and climate change, such strains not only protect the food supply, they keep desert gardeners of all heritages supplied with super-adapted plants to push the growing season through into brutal heat of summer.

The online catalog and print version offer over 500 varieties of plants, many of them available nowhere else. This catalog includes some of the most unique varieties of indigenous corn and is the source for super-popular Glass Gem, a variety considered the most colorful of all. This is also the best source for truly outstanding amaranth and other unusual crops such as cotton, tobacco, and indigenous squash. Contact the organization at (520) 622-0830 or at NativeSeeds.org.

HOPI RED DYE AMARANTH NATIVE SEEDS/SEARCH

The beautiful plant can grow 6 feet tall with a 1- to 2-inch-long inflorescence and dark reddish-green leaves. Young tender leaves are excellent in salads and the black seeds are also edible. The Hopi make a scarlet natural food dye from the flower bract to color piki bread. Originally collected in Lower Moenkopi.

HEAT AND DROUGHT VARIETIES BY REGION

TOMATO

High Desert: Rosso Sicilian, Tartar of Mongolistan, Turkish Striped Monastary, Homestead 24, Porter Improved, Costulo Genovese, Tropic, Native Sun

Low Desert: Thessaloniki, Solar Flare, Abu Rawan, Basrawya, Moneymaker, Nineveh, Omar's Lebanese, Ciudad Victoria, Punta Banda

Mountains (short season): Siletz, Legend, Beaverlodge, Glacier, Northern Delight, Stupice, Fizz (cherry), Nova (roma), Prescott Heirloom

Coastal: Oregon Spring, Gill's All-Purpose, Punta Banda, San Francisco Fog, Super Tasty, Viva Italia

Inland Valley: Arkansas Traveler, Brandywine, Eva Purple Ball, Marvel Striped, Purple Calabash, Ozark Pink

BELL/SWEET PEPPER

High Desert: Jimmy Nardello Italian, Corno di Toro Giallo, Ordono, Jupiter Red Bell

Low Desert: Criolla de Cocina, Syrian Three Sided Pepper, Doux D'Espagne (Spanish Mammoth), Arroz con Pollo, Del Arbol de Baja California Sur Chile

Mountains (short season): Sheepnose Pimento, Bulgarian Ratund, King of the North, Nambe Supreme Chile, Isleta Chile, Chimayo Chile

Coastal: New Ace, Yolo Wonder, Anaheim, Yellow Wax

Inland Valley: Big Bertha, California Wonder, Marconi, Sweet Banana, Anaheim

EGGPLANT

High Desert: Gbogname Collared, Syrian Stuffing, Turkish Orange, Edirne Purple Striped, Auburgine Burkina

Low Desert: Kazakhstan, Rosita, Aswad, Florida High Bush

Mountains (short season): Ichiban

Coastal: Ichiban, Black Beauty, Dusky, Rosa Bianco

Inland Valley: Ping Tung Long, Thai Green, Listada de Gandia

SQUASH

High Desert: Sunburst Patty Pan, Lebanese White Bush Marrow, Tatume Zucchini

Low Desert: Dixie Crookneck, Tatume Zucchini, Iran, Costata Romanesco Zucchini

Mountains (short season): White Bush Scallop Patty Pan, BC-2 Hybrid Zucchini, Early Prolific Straightneck

Coastal: Table King Acorn, Lemon, Golden, Striata D'Italia

Inland Valley: Green Stripes Cuchaw (winter), Cocozelle Zucchini, Dark Star Zucchini, Black Beauty Zucchini

CUCUMBER

High Desert: Lemon, Armenian, Beit Alpha, General Lee

Low Desert: Armenian, Lemon, Poona Kheera, Summer Dance

Mountains (short season): Marketmore 76, Marketer, Morden Early #382

Coastal: Straight Eight, Salad Bush, Liberty Hybrid, County Fair 83

Inland Valley: General Lee, Lemon, Edmonson, Suyo Long

PEAS/BEANS

High Desert: Oregon Sugar Pod II Snow Pea, Rattlesnake Green Bean, Royalty Purple Pod, Yard Long Bean, Chinese Green Noodle Bean

Low Desert: Blue Speckled Tepary Bean, Blue Coco Bean, Venture Bean, Asparagus Pea, Gita Yard Long Bean

Mountains (short season): Provider Snap Bean, Renegade Bush Bean, Jade Bean Bush Bean, Alaska Pea, Oregon Sugar Pod II Snow Pea, Contender Snap Bean

Coastal: Super Sugar Snaps Pea, Cherokee Wax Bean, Tendergreen Bush Bean, Butter Crisp Bush Bean, Snowbird Pea, Wando Pea

Inland Valley: Oregon Sugar Pod II Snow Pea, Ideal Market Bean, Cherokee Trail of Tears, Golden Sweet Snow Pea, Chinese Green Noodle Bean, Landreth Stringless Bean

BRASSICA TRIBE

High Desert: Purple of Sicily Cauliflower, Lacinato Kale

Low Desert: Purple of Sicily Cauliflower, Lacinato Kale

Mountains (short season): Red Russian Kale, Solstice Broccoli, Earliana

Coastal: Bacalan De Rennes Cabbage, Nero Di Toscana, Green Goliath Broccoli

ROOT TRIBE

High Desert: Bull's Blood Beet, Flat of Egypt Beet

Low Desert: Chioggia Beet, Flat of Egypt Beet

Mountains (short season): Early Wonder Beet, Botardy #552

GREENS

High Desert: Jericho Romaine, Tatsoi (Asian), Bak Choy (Asian), Pac Choy (Asian), Australian Yellowleaf Lettuce, Hopi Red Dye Amaranth

Low Desert: Nevada Lettuce, Tatsoi (Asian), Bak Choy (Asian), Pac Choy (Asian), Gold Rush Lettuce, Perpetual Swiss Chard

Mountains (short season): Tatsoi (Asian), Bak Choy (Asian), Pac Choy (Asian), Space Hybrid Spinach, Sierra Lettuce

Coastal: Tatsoi (Asian), Bak Choy (Asian), Pac Choy (Asian)

Inland Valley: Freckles Romaine, Merveille Des Quatre Saisons Lettuce, Slobolt Lettuce, Green Oakleaf Lettuce, Perpetual Swiss Chard, Canton Bok Asian Green

MELON

High Desert: Hopi Casaba, Melon De Castilla, San Juan Native, Jumanos Watermelon, Tohono O'odham Yellow Meated Watermelon

Low Desert: Old Woman's Knees Pima Melon, Mayo Minol, Isleta Pueblo, Hopi Red Kawayvatnga Watermelon, Desert King Watermelon

Coastal: Earliequeen, Halona

Inland Valley: Planter's Jumbo, Small Persian

CORN

High Desert: Anasazi Sweet, Daymon Morgan's Kentucky, Butcher, Hopi Blue Flour Hopi Pink, Painted Mountain Flour

Low Desert: Silver Queen, Daymon Morgan's Kentucky, Country Gentleman

Mountains (short season): Yukon Chief

Coastal: Northern Extra Sweet

Inland Valley: Oaxacan Green Dent, Black Aztec, Silver Queen Hybrid Sweet, Tennessee Red Cob, How Sweet It Is

When growing vegetables with as little water as possible, success depends on selecting the right varieties that are naturally adapted to withstanding minimal humidity. The world is full of little known private landrace strains of common vegetables that maintain an edge over garden varieties. You'll soon realize how important more lengthy descriptions can be to discovering the stalwart strains that are so different from cool, moisture-loving versions of the very same vegetable. The real rewards come when you find a whole new kind of vegetable to grow, one that may be little known outside isolated desert villages. This makes you an integral part of a collective effort to expand diversity and support sustainable agriculture through continuous cultivation of a vanishing heritage.

CHAPTER 8

Seeds and Seedlings

Start where you are. Use what you have.
Do what you can.
—ARTHUR ASHE

In an arid climate, the most challenging aspect of growing vegetables is getting them started. Whether you sow directly in-ground or start your seeds ahead of time indoors, they all must eventually face the heat, wind, and low humidity. Well-started plants produce larger root systems better able to withstand the rigors of weather. Any plant not at the peak of health becomes more vulnerable in the low-water garden or in the extremes of the desert. The old expression rings true: a garden well begun is indeed half done.

SEED OR SEEDLING?

All vegetables can either be direct-sown into the soil or started ahead in containers and planted out later on. The real question is, why go to the trouble to start plants in pots? Why not just sow all seed directly in the ground? Here are answers that help you make the best decision for your garden, your climate, and your lifestyle.

Extending the Growing Season

Where the growing season is shorter, such as high-and-dry communities of the Rockies and Sierra Nevadas, vegetables may fail to ripen properly before the frost comes. If they do ripen, there's often no time for a second or third picking.

Vegetables with a long life span that produce their crops over many consecutive weeks rather than all at once won't have time to reach their full potential. Starting long–life span vegetables, such as tomatoes, weeks ahead of time in the warmth of a greenhouse or indoors will help them ripen their first fruits earlier and allow more time for additional yields.

Divide the Season in Two

In the desert, the growing season is split by a brutal midsummer dormant season and a "second spring" falls in late September. Here, crops produce very early, then some hunker down for summer and start up again in early fall. Others simply die in the heat. In the first season, tomato seedlings are planted out in late January or early February in the low desert. The earlier these plants get started, the earlier the harvest begins since it's duration will be terminated by the soaring temperatures of desert summer. New tomato plants can be started indoors during the height of summer to plant out fresh in the fall. In the high desert, there is also a split in the season, but with later spring frost, starting early extends the season, increasing pre-summer yield before high temperatures interfere with flowering. Here, too, new plants can go out in the fall to produce well into the holidays.

More Controlled Moisture Levels

The first few days after germination are the most vulnerable in the life of a vegetable plant. Out in the garden, it can be difficult to maintain steady moisture levels in dry conditions where temperatures fluctuate radically. Hot days literally suck moisture out of plant tissues and the soil at a startling rate, and unless you use a cloche or row covers, it can be nearly impossible to keep seedlings moist enough. For this reason, starting plants indoors or in a greenhouse is the best way to nurse them through those first days in an evenly moist environment. Even indoors in low-humidity climates, you may need further enclosure so the moisture in the soil actually humidifies the air around each plant. A simple solution is to keep your seedling pots in a deeper plastic box, then attach a sheet of plastic food wrap over the top for a miniature indoor greenhouse. Once the root system gets established, gradually open the top a little more each day to help seedlings adjust to drier air.

PROBLEMS WITH STORE-BOUGHT SEEDLINGS

While buying potted seedlings can speed up or simplify your planting process, it's not always the best way to go. Here's why:

DIVERSITY: In the previous chapter we looked at how specialized varieties developed in desertlike climates are best for growing with minimal water. Seedlings sold in chain stores are usually the most common, general-purpose vegetable varieties, with few heirlooms. The only way to grow specialized varieties for a drought-resistant garden is to start them from seed yourself.

ACCLIMATION: Seedlings grown in large greenhouses with softened lighting, humid air, and specialized irrigation aren't ready to inhabit a low-water garden. When sold in the desert, you may notice that all the seedlings are kept under shade cloth or even under a solid overhead structure to protect them from the elements. The younger seedlings will require a more gradual period to acclimate to your home garden so they're not stressed by the sudden shift from optimal greenhouses or full shade to hot inland valley or desert with extreme UV levels.

TIP: Certain crops are rarely started in pots. Root crops can be too easily damaged in transplanting, or if the tap root of a carrot hits the bottom of the container it can take a turn and never straighten out. Fast-growing seedlings such as squash are so quick there's no real benefit to pre-starting. Plants like corn and lettuce that are grown in large quantities would be too time consuming to start ahead as well.

USE BIODEGRADABLE POTS

Peat pots are made of compressed ground peat, so the entire container with its seedling can be planted in the ground—a great benefit for eliminating transplant shock in hot, dry climates.

Starting vegetables in pots is easier if you use the right kind of container. Peat pots, or cow pots made of shaped manure, are ideal because you don't have to remove the plant and soil from a plastic container. You simply plant the whole pot and it decomposes on its own. This helps your seedlings adapt more quickly to their new home because roots aren't disturbed or exposed to the air during transplanting. The peat itself is well-known to absorb and hold water for a long time, so the developing root ball is separated from drier outer soil by this damp yet porous barrier. Peat pots are key to minimizing transplant shock and simplify the process so much that anyone can do it with 100 percent success.

EASY ENCLOSURE FOR DRY CLIMATES

In dry climates, it can be challenging to keep potting soil consistently moist for seeds to germinate. A good solution is the clear, plastic-lidded box used to sell lettuce, roasted chickens, and take-out food. The larger deep lettuce boxes are among the best because seedlings can grow taller before they reach the roof.

TIP: Large-scale gardeners always save their plastic seedling containers to start new crops. Whenever you reuse a container, wash it well, then dip it in a 10 percent bleach solution to kill any diseases or pest eggs remaining from the previous plant.

Each container allows you to start your seed in six or more 2- or 3-inch pots so you may need a few of them to solve the problem of an ultra-low-humidity climate. When seed is first sown, keep the container closed up tight to maintain even soil moisture and warmth. After plants germinate, open the top each day for a few minutes to freshen the air. Open the top for a bit longer each day to harden plants off to drier conditions gradually.

To water the plants, simply pour tepid water into the bottom of the container and the pots will wick up the moisture. This prevents dislodging the seed or tiny roots, which might happen when you apply water to the surface. When seedlings become too large, leave the cover open or cut off the lid. The last step is to move the containers outdoors during the day in a sheltered location to stimulate growth and help them adapt to wind before finally planting out into the garden.

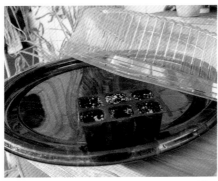

Plastic party trays are large enough to hold a number of recycled plastic six-pack plant pots.

Use what you have first—a recycled tin roasting pan holds recycled pots with sheet plastic or a thick plastic bag clipped to the top with clothespin.

Recycled plastic six-packs become a super moist temporary germination environment using plastic wrap.

A blueberry box is repurposed to a seed-starting mini greenhouse.

ROOTING MEDIUM PAYS

The biggest challenge with starting seeds in pots is avoiding a disease such as damping-off, which afflicts newly sprouted seedlings. The genesis of many seedling pests and diseases can be the soil you use to germinate the seeds. That's why it's best to purchase rooting medium, which is a super-fine sterile material designed for starting seed-grown plants. The woody matter in ordinary potting soil often carries fungus spores that can flourish in the warm, moist conditions needed to start seed. Rooting medium is light enough for new roots to penetrate easily and it won't pack down when watered. It's wise to moisten the rooting medium in advance of planting. Using the bag it comes in or an open waterproof box, sprinkle with water and mix with your hands until the medium feels evenly moist but not wet. Start with small amounts of water, then add more until the consistency feels good. This ensures uniform dampness without dry pockets that resist moisture when you water later on.

CLOCHE RECONSIDERED: TRY RECYCLED

A cloche is a miniature greenhouse used for seedlings right after transplanting outdoors into the garden. It also can be set up over ground where seed is newly sown to create an atmosphere that protects the seedling from dehydration. A glass cloche is traditionally used in colder climates to protect the transplants from late frost so planting may begin earlier. A cloche can help your young transplants too, but in a different way. It is the best way to maintain a humid environment and protect from desiccating wind or a heat wave. Make a free, recycled cloche by cutting the bottom off a translucent plastic gallon milk or water jug. The clouded plastic filters UV rays, protecting the plant from sunburn. It also retains moisture rising out of the soil, holding it around the plant

A cloche is a cover used out in the garden to protect young seedlings from late frost, or to maintain a more moist environment for them to get a stronger start.

while blocking wind. The jug lid can be removed to allow super-heated air to rise up and out of this mini-greenhouse. You can melt holes in the plastic with a hot screwdriver to allow you to stake it in place against wind movement with a piece of U-shaped coat hanger, drip-system pins, bamboo stake, or repurposed twigs.

SOWING WITH A DRIP SYSTEM

Chapter 5 details all the ways we can water plants using a drip system, and your watering system is integral to the way you sow the garden. Before you plant, check the recommended spacing on the seed packet. Then choose tubing with emitters spaced at the same intervals so you can sow each seed directly next to the water source. When using ¼-inch tubing with pre-installed (inline) emitters, the emitters will be spaced every 6, 9, or 12 inches. Larger ½-inch tubing will have emitters every 9, 12, 18, 24, or 36 inches.

Even if the system isn't up-and-running yet, set this line out and pin it in place as your planting guide. Planting this way will make sure every drop of water is delivered directly into the root zone.

SEED PROBLEMS: DON'T GET DISCOURAGED

Starting plants from seed seems so easy that even a first grader can do it. Bringing that sprout to mature bearing age is another matter entirely. There are many ways that your efforts may fail, but never give up. Failure is merely a more painful way to learn how to do it right. Experienced gardeners all agree that you learn more from what you do wrong than what you do right. Simply start again, taking what you've learned into consideration. The vast majority of seed-starting failures are listed below, with details about their causes and lessons.

Always date any seed you save, buy, or receive, so you'll know how old it is in the future, which can have a big impact on germination rates.

Seed Is Too Old or Damaged

Always buy fresh seed each year. If you are saving your seed from last year's garden, be sure to store it properly and mark the container with a date. While in storage, moisture or pantry insects can kill the seed even if it doesn't look any different. The small price of fresh seed is far more affordable than the time it takes you to plant it twice.

EASY SEED GERMINATION TEST

If you're not sure if your seed is still viable, here's an easy germination test. Do it in the kitchen with a dinner plate and paper towels. Wet four squares of paper towel and wring out so they are still quite moist but not sopping wet. Lay two layers on the plate, scatter the seeds on the surface, then lay the other two layers on top of them. Place the plate in a dark cupboard, because seed needs darkness to sprout. The best cupboard will be the one over your stove or oven to provide enough warmth to make seed sprout more quickly. Check the moisture content each day and wet gently if towels dry out. Each type of seed germinates at a different rate. If you don't see a root emerging within the span of time for that crop, it's not viable. If you don't know how many days to germination, allow up to two weeks for the test.

TIP: If you don't have a seed packet or any other guide to planting depth, there's a general rule of thumb that works for most types of seed. Plant a seed at a depth 3 times its diameter. Using this system, 1/16-inch broccoli seed should be planted just 3/16 inches deep!

Seed Is Planted Too Deep

Some seed is highly sensitive to its depth in the soil. Some types need only a scattering of soil grains on top because they require some light to germinate. With these, even slightly deeper planting can completely eliminate germination. For others, depth can cause the seed to rot before it has a chance to grow. Be attentive to planting depth designated on the seed packet and stick to it.

AVERAGE GERMINATION RATES OF COMMON VEGETABLE SEED

Note: Range of days indicates shorter germination rates in warmer soils.

SEED	RATE
Beans	7 to 10 days
Cabbage group	5 to 10 days
Melons	5 to 10 days
Carrots	12 to 15 days
Corn	7 to 10 days
Cucumbers	7 to 10 days
Eggplant	10 to 12 days
Lettuce	7 to 10 days
Peas	1 to 2 weeks
Peppers	10 to 14 days
Squash	1 to 2 weeks
Tomatoes	1 to 2 weeks

Soil Is Saturated

When starting seed in containers indoors, there may be minimal evaporation. It's easy to water too often under these conditions, particularly with seed that takes a long time to germinate. Overwatering causes water to displace oxygen that should exist in tiny gaps in the soil. This creates an anaerobic (oxygen-free) condition that is ripe for some undesirable microorganisms to flourish.

Good seed will germinate readily if conditions are right with ideal soil temperature, even moisture, and good drainage so seed won't rot in cold wet ground.

Whether the seed root dies due to lack of oxygen or from a pathogen thriving in saturated soil, you may never know.

There Is Inadequate Drainage

Soil saturation is the hidden killer of seeds and seedlings. That's why it's important to use containers that are very well-drained. This problem crops up when recycled containers such as yogurt cups are used to start seed. Too often just one small hole is made in the bottom for drainage. It is far better to have three or more clean holes so if one clogs up, drainage is still assured.

Soil Has Dry Pockets

Seed starting media that contains a lot of peat sometimes can hold invisible dry pockets. When you water, moisture moves through the damp peat but does not penetrate the dry pocket. If your seed is in the dry pocket, it won't sprout. This is why it's important to make sure the entire mass is thoroughly saturated right after you sow the seed to eliminate the potential for these invisible problems.

Soil Is Too Cold

Indoors or out, many summer vegetables require soil temperatures from 60 to 75 degrees F. Planting into soil or a seed-sowing medium below 60 degrees F may prevent the seeds from sprouting or growing. When it's too cold, the seed just sits there absorbing moisture, but it won't grow. This will cause the seed to rot before it germinates. Only by knowing just how long that plant requires to germinate, (see Average Germination Rates chart, page 137), will you know if each plant is delayed by cold soil or not.

When seed is sown too early and soil or climate is too cold, the seed may germinate and then the

The benefit of saving your nursery containers is the ability to transplant from a sprouting tray to smaller pots, so seedlings can form a healthy root system before being moved outdoors.

tiny seedling just sits there waiting for the heat. In the meantime every crawling insect pest that encounters that seedling will take a bite or chew it down to the ground. If planted under normal warm conditions, the seedling usually shoots out of the ground and grows well beyond the reach of the crawling pests within just a few days. This is why it's best to err on the side of sowing too late rather than risk having all your early efforts undone by the bugs. It also explains why starting seed indoors in climates that experience late frost is often the best choice.

When starting a garden from seeds or seedlings, it's vital to keep moisture availability front and center in the droughty garden. There are many ways to achieve a gentle place to start life, whether it's under a row cover or a cloche, in a cold frame or greenhouse, or just in a box covered with plastic wrap. Sowing a plant from seed and nursing it through those first few weeks is one of the most important skills you'll ever learn. When growing in extreme heat or where water is precious, problem solving becomes a big part of that skill set.

CHAPTER 9

Seasonal Crop Guide

Out on Salisbury Plain of England, the great circular of pillars of Stonehenge can be considered one of the earliest man-made calendars. It was designed in the late Bronze Age for people who sought a guide to the solar travels through the year. On specific dates, the sun rises and sets at key points on this great ring of stone, noting with certainty the exact days of the solar year that became the hallmarks of our agrarian world.

While our days are charted by printed pages of a calendar, the world of plants and farming is far better dictated by seasons themselves. The winter of 2013–2014 was one of the warmest in recent history in the far north. Similarly, 2014–2015 is colder earlier than recent history for the same area. These kinds of anomalies are not part of our printed calendar, and yet such variations happen all the time. Farmers learned long ago to become superconscious of the subtle and sometimes not-so-subtle changes to the annual cycles by planting and harvesting earlier or later when the natural signs proved it beneficial.

The four seasons are defined by day length, which is the number of hours between sunrise and sunset. In tropical climates, day length is often the chief governing factor of plant longevity because there's no frost to end their life cycle or initiate true dormancy. This is important for those in the low tropical desert because vegetables are grown over the mild winter season, which is defined strictly by day length.

WHY DAY LENGTH MATTERS

Summer vegetables are annual plants that must complete their life cycle in the span of a single growing season. You can divide this cycle into two primary growth mechanisms. The first part is the vegetative growth cycle, where plants grow large enough to reproduce. This occurs between the winter solstice and the summer solstice as days are growing longer. After the summer solstice, these plants sense shortening day lengths, which shifts them into flower and seed production. Remember, a tomato is really just the vehicle for that plant to reproduce by seed.

Leaf and root crops are a bit different. They bolt and flower only at the end of life. Often you can see a change in them right after June 21, proving just how sensitive they are to this pivotal point.

This is important in the low-water garden because we recognize the natural responses of plants to these changes. All too often, novice gardeners see a change in their plants and assume it's caused by the heat of summer when it's wholly day-length related. They react by watering more heavily when it's not necessarily. To conserve water, it's vital to know what's going on with the plants and why, so you can avoid waste trying to "cure" a natural response.

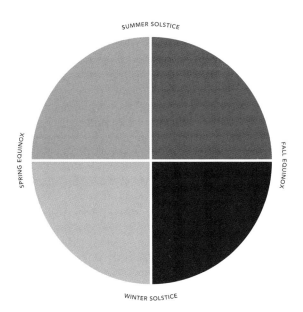

UNDERSTANDING YOUR YEAR

The fundamental way of breaking down your gardening year is to recognize the four quarters of the solar year.

Spring Equinox, March 21: First Day of Spring

The equinox designates the point where day and night are of equal length. This marks the halfway point between the winter solstice and summer solstice. The spring equinox is the time of rebirth of all life.

Summer Solstice, June 21: First Day of Summer

At this point, the span of daylight will be longer than any other day of the year. Sunset on this day aligns the sun opposite the point of the winter solstice at Stonehenge. It is a date that shifts plants from vegetative growth to reproductive growth, because after this day, each period of daylight grows incrementally shorter.

WARM-SEASON CROPS

These vegetables germinate at soil temperatures from 60 to 75 degrees F, and depend on heat to flower and produce fruit. Examples: tomato, squash, and beans.

Autumn Equinox, September 21: First Day of Autumn

This is the opposite of the spring equinox, and again, day and night are of equal length. This is the death knell for annual plants that must hurry and set seed before frost. It also signals to deciduous plants that time has come to shed their foliage.

COOL-SEASON CROPS

These vegetables germinate in cooler soils averaging about 40 degrees F or warmer, and prefer cooler temperatures to produce edible foliage. These crops bolt at 90 degrees F, but they also are stimulated by long day length. Examples: kale, lettuce, and chard.

Winter Solstice, December 21: First Day of Winter

This solstice marks the turning point when days cease to grow shorter and begin to lengthen imperceptibly toward spring. This day has the shortest span of daylight and the longest period of darkness. At Stonehenge, the sun sets this day at the point opposite that of the summer solstice.

SEASONS OF THE TEMPERATE GARDEN

The temperate garden reflects the seasons of most climatic regions. In water-conservation gardens it's key to recognize the first cool season for growing, which can begin in winter where soils don't freeze, or early spring when the soil is damp and remains so consistently for a few months. This is the best time to expand your crop production by sowing seeds for cool-season crops in fall or during winter in moderate climates such as the Pacific Northwest, to exploit the moisture availability. It's a good idea to prepare these planting areas and sow seed in the late fall so you won't be mucking around in the mud, which can compact clayey soils and limit water penetration or drainage.

COUNTERINTUITIVE SEASONS OF THE LOW DESERT

The low desert has its own unique seasons that stymie gardeners from other regions because the winters are so mild. Areas such as Palm Springs and Tucson are technically tropical desert without much cold and only a few mornings of brief dawn frost. However, occasional years have proven considerably colder.

TIP: December is the best time to start your warm-season crops indoors to be prepared for late January or February outdoor planting opportunities.

Late Winter

After January frost passes, consider this a true early spring. It's a narrow window of time to start the growing season that extends until the heat of June, so timing is crucial. Sow both cool- and warm-season crops at this time or set out seedlings purchased or started indoors. Spring-planted tomatoes set out now will grow quickly with the lengthening days and increasing heat for harvest into July. These dates may vary from year to year depending on how hot the month of May proves to be. If your garden experiences super-high heat in May, tomatoes will cease flowering, which prevents new fruit formation.

Spring

Consider the equinox the last date for planting vegetable crops in the low desert. When planting in spring, use very mature plants grown to larger sizes so they are far enough along to withstand the heat and still set a crop. Short-term crops such as greens and radishes can still be grown now.

Summer

The end of June until September should be considered the dormant season. Even the most heat-loving vegetables have trouble withstanding temperatures well over 110 degrees F for weeks at a time. However, the low desert is a curious place, where microclimates can make a huge difference. Often surprises occur in protected courtyards and side yards where buildings can so modify the climate that plants manage to do very well with enough water. These are exceptions, however. Use the summer solstice as the official end of the season for vegetable gardening in the low desert.

Fall

The low desert can remain quite hot until the end of October, when true fall sets in. October is a busy planting and sowing month for both warm- and cool-season crops. This is about the only time to grow lettuce, Asian vegetables, and cole crops without concerns for premature bolting due to hot day temperatures over the holidays and January. Tomato seedlings planted in the fall will grow quickly, but slow down or stop altogether during the solstice, when they need some protection such as row covers, a bed sheet, or a Planket (a lightweight plant cover) on frosty nights. Keep an eye on NOAA weather forecasts to let you know if the coming night will be cold enough to lay out your crop covers. Fall-planted tomatoes protected over winter will be well-established to ripen earlier than tomato seedlings planted out in January or early February.

SEASONS OF THE HIGH DESERT

The term high desert applies to most parts of the inland west, including Las Vegas, the Great Basin, and the Southwest beyond the influence of tropical monsoons. Weather in this massive region will be highly variable depending on elevation and microclimate, so it may take a year or two to learn exactly when and what to plant in your locale. Winter gardens on south-facing slopes will be far warmer than those in low-lying areas with cold air drainage. In high desert, the summer growing season is split to allow a brief dormancy during the hottest days of July and August.

TIP: In the high desert, sow snow and snap peas in winter or follow the traditional St. Patrick's Day date for sowing because these vine crops do best during cool conditions. With days heating up quickly, early sowing helps keep your production within the ideal temperature range. Once dry heat and wind signal seasonal change, these plants have a hard time maintaining internal moisture, causing leaves to wither, viral diseases to thrive, and edible pods to become tough or stringy.

Spring

Frost lingers late in the high desert and heat comes early so the spring planting window can be quite narrow. Planting in the open happens around the first of May, as it does in many other temperate regions. However, the season for sowing cool-season crops can begin much earlier with row covers and other frost-protection devices. In some years with a mild winter, row covers can help fall-sown plants overwinter for a big jump on spring harvest. Plants grown indoors, in a greenhouse, or in a cold frame can reach a large size by May, so they will be much further along when planted out. Tomatoes planted this way will mature and produce a first crop by early July, but growth will soon slow or stop when temperatures rise above 95 degrees F. The plants remain hunkered down until the end of August, when they start up again. Gardeners often trim off the dried-out remnants of the early season growth to stimulate new foliage replacement.

Summer

Consider July and August the "depths" of summer when some crops fail and others simply stop growing and fruiting. Do not consider all these plants dead because some are just resting to waiting out the heat. Maintain minimal irrigation to prevent the roots from dying. In September, plants recognize the shorter days and lower temperature to grow again, producing until Christmas.

Fall

Autumn in the high desert can be one of the most productive seasons, with extensive periods of moderate growing conditions. Often this is the only time summer squash thrives. This is the season for peppers, which return from summer hiatus to produce well into the holidays. Though day length does discourage some growth, plants thrive in the warm days and cool evenings of extended warm, dry falls. Sow fast-growing summer squash in September along with all your cool-season crops so that they are well along by the time frost hits. Hardy plants like kale and winter greens will take some frost, or simply use row covers to carry your harvest of fresh greens into spring.

WHAT IS COLD AIR DRAINAGE?

This term relates to the way cold air moves on the land. Cold air is heavier than warm air so, like propane, gas, or water, it seeks the lowest elevation to pool. This is the reason why a higher elevation home site can experience less frost than a home 500 feet below it. In some hill country locations, you can stand outside at dawn or after sunset and actually feel an air exchange occur. This phenomenon allows cold air from the high country to flow down slope to the valley floor, where it displaces the air warmed up by a full day's solar radiation. Warm air rises higher on the slope to create much warmer night temperatures there. This demonstrates how gardens on hills can produce far longer than those in some valleys, so don't assume that, just because you are higher, your growing season is shorter.

TRIBAL GUIDE TO VEGETABLES FOR DESERT, DROUGHT, AND WATER-CONSERVATION GARDENS

Many of our favorite vegetables can be grouped into families, but it's simpler to think of them as members of a tribe. People in tribes follow the same cultural practices and are often closely linked genetically. When plants belong to the same tribe they often respond to similar conditions. Understanding these tribal affiliations helps you to learn more in less time and discover the relationships of these plants for a logical approach to their selection and care. Tribes help you zero in on those vegetables that originate in more arid or warm parts of the world and thus will make better candidates for desert and low-humidity conditions.

Nightshade Tribe (Solanaceae Family)

This tribe loves heat because plants must flower and be pollinated before the edible fruit parts form. This is true of all but the potato, which prefers cooler temperatures because only the tuberous roots are edible.

Their place of origin explains why nightshade vegetables are such a staple in gardens and cuisine of hot, dry lands around the world. Most originated in arid parts of the New World, primarily Mexico and south into Peru. Because potatoes originated in the cool but arid Andes Mountains, they aren't as heat-loving as the pepper and tomato. The eggplant is the only Old World nightshade; it originated in the Indian subcontinent, where it is known as aubergine. Virtually all these plants were taken to Europe from the Americas, then spread into Asia Minor, the

Middle East, and North Africa, where they were developed and selected for greater production, increased flavor, and diverse characteristics. This demonstrates that the nightshade vegetables will adapt to lower water levels than other vegetables that originate in cooler climates. However, many varieties of these vegetables were specially bred to grow in cooler, rainy climates of Europe, particularly the potato, which found a home in temperate Ireland.

Tomato

TYPE: Annual fruit. Actually a perennial grown as an annual.

VARIATIONS: Determinate varieties produce their fruit all at once for canning and sauce. Indeterminate varieties flower and fruit over a much longer period for better production in low desert and mild winter regions. Dwarf tomatoes are best for containers.

TRELLIS: Prefab tomato tower, wire field fencing, or welded wire mesh rolled into a tube.

Tomatoes are the most frequently grown nightshade vegetable.

EXPOSURE: Full sun. Afternoon shade in the low desert.

SEASON: Warm.

PLANTING METHOD: Direct-sow seed, start ahead in containers or buy nursery-grown seedlings.

CULTIVATION: Tomatoes root along their stems, so how you plant can influence the extent of the rooting potential. This is vital for low-water gardens where drought resistance can be maximized by promoting more expansive rooting. Plant seedlings extra deep or lay them on their sides in a trench to stimulate roots along the buried portion of the stem. The larger root system results in a more-water efficient plant that can access moisture from a much larger area of soil.

FROST TOLERANCE: None.

PESTS: Tomato hornworm (treat with Bt) and whitefly (treat with insecticidal soap).

DISEASES: Many. Be sure to rotate your tomato plants into different beds to prevent disease buildup in your soil. Sandy desert soil can experience incurable root knot nematode infestations that thrive in porous ground with low organic matter.

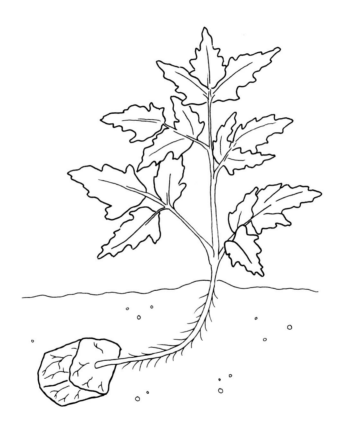

Dig a trench about 3 inches deep and lay the seedling down, so the root ball and stem are evenly covered with 2 inches of soil. This encourages new roots to form all along the length of the stem for a greater moisture uptake ability, which enhances drought resistance.

Tomatillo

TYPE: Bushy annual fruit from Mexico.

TRELLIS: None.

EXPOSURE: Full sun.

SEASON: Warm.

PLANTING METHOD: Direct sow seed in-ground. Warm soil for germination.

CULTIVATION: Sow outdoors 5 weeks after last frost, indoors 2 weeks prior to last frost.

FROST TOLERANCE: None.

PESTS: Same as tomato.

DISEASES: Blight, wilt.

> **TIP:** Where disease is common, select modern tomato varieties bred for resistance to specific diseases. This will be designated by abbreviations after the varietal name. Common viral designations for tomatoes are *F* for fusarium wilt resistance, *V* for verticillium wilt, *L* for grey leaf spot, and *N* for nematodes, a type of root-damaging round worm.

Pepper

TYPE: Annual fruit, though some are short-lived perennials.

VARIATIONS: Sweet or hot.

TRELLIS: Stake plants as needed for support. Prune back overly tall plants for stronger branching structure.

EXPOSURE: Full sun. Afternoon shade in low desert.

SEASON: Warm; best where growing season is very long.

Native Seed/SEARCH offers traditional chiles of the desert Southwest and northern Mexico.

For small gardens and containers, explore the dwarf forms of peppers that produce well in little space.

PLANTING METHOD: Seed or seedlings, in the ground or in containers.

CULTIVATION: Start seedlings 10 weeks before last frost date. Sow earlier in pots where season is short to maximize yields. Plant outdoors only after night temperatures are at least 55 degrees F.

FROST TOLERANCE: None.

PESTS: Will be vulnerable to tomato hornworm and small sucking insects such as whiteflies.

DISEASES: Select resistant varieties.

Eggplant

Japanese eggplants feature lighter weight fruit than large stuffing eggplant and thus require less staking.

TYPE: Annual fruit.

VARIATIONS: Large, Italian stuffing types, or smaller, egg-shaped or elongated Asian types.

TRELLIS: Staking is common when large stuffing types tend to weight branches and may pull over the entire plant.

EXPOSURE: Full sun.

SEASON: Warm. Prefers night temperature at least 65 degrees F.

PLANTING METHOD: Start seeds in containers 10 weeks before last frost.

CULTIVATION: Plant seedlings in the garden after last frost and soil is warm.

FROST TOLERANCE: None.

PESTS: Caterpillars, aphids, whiteflies.

DISEASES: Rotate plants into different beds every year to fight blight and wilt.

Potato

TYPE: Cool-season tuberous root perennial, grown as annual crop.

VARIATIONS: Standard or fingerling. Smooth or russet skin.

TRELLIS: May be grown in wire tube cage or stacked auto tires for vertical space-saver.

EXPOSURE: Full sun. Requires protection from dry wind in the desert.

SEASON: Cool. Early spring crop in warm climates.

PLANTING METHOD: Potatoes are grown from chunks or mini-tubers called seed potatoes. Any organic potato can be cut into chunks to start new plants. Each chunk must have at least one eye, preferably two or more. Commercially grown supermarket potatoes may be treated with germination inhibitors.

CULTIVATION: Grow in ground or in pots. Popular wine barrel crop. Requires mounding soil around base of plant to protect developing potatoes from sunlight, which turns them green and makes the skins poisonous. Hilling up potatoes also provides more root zone to encourage a larger yield.

FROST TOLERANCE: None.

In hot, dry conditions it's best to plant seed potatoes in the moist, damp ground during the winter, so harvest occurs before extreme summer heat.

As you add soil to cover the roots of these potato plants, they produce more foliage working their way upward, maximizing the crop produced in just a few square feet of space.

PESTS: Few if grown in early season, before insect populations rise.

DISEASES: Avoid by planting only certified disease-free seed potatoes.

Brassica Tribe (Brassicaceae Family)

With this tribe, some produce only edible leaves, as with kale; in others, such as broccoli, the flower buds are the tasty part. These are the workhorse plants in cooler climates with shorter seasons.

Cole crops, also known as cruciferous vegetables, are members of the cabbage family and are all closely related. Since they originate in the Old World, they have been cultivated for millennia, so that many variations evolved into our diverse crops of today. What binds this group is the fact that they thrive in cooler, damp climates. Brassicas may not be grown during the summer months in the desert or in any hot climate because they tend to bolt and flower too quickly. Heat also causes them to suffer from wooly aphids. However, they may prove highly productive in very warm, low-desert winter gardens. These vegetables are grown in early spring or fall in most regions, except in mild coastal zones with strong maritime influence where they thrive even into summer, such as in California's famous "June Gloom" conditions.

Cabbage

TYPE: Biennial grown as annual crop.

VARIATIONS: Green or purple color.

TRELLIS: No.

EXPOSURE: Full sun, coastal and mountain. Afternoon shade, inland and desert, or full sun in winter.

SEASON: Cool. Winter crop in the desert.

PLANTING METHOD: Seed.

CULTIVATION: For hot climates, start cabbage in containers well in advance, so once they're planted out, heads have time to fully mature before high heat and dry conditions prevail.

FROST TOLERANCE: Marginal.

PESTS: Worms, maggots.

DISEASES: Minimal.

Cabbage sown in the fall will thrive for most of the winter in milder climates.

Kale and Collards

TYPE: Biennial grown as annual crop. Closely related to cabbage. Collards are considered a different form of kale, more tolerant of heat so they are traditionally grown in the Deep South.

VARIATIONS: Curled or flat leaf forms.

TRELLIS: No.

ROW COVERS: Yes, for kale.

EXPOSURE: Full sun coastal and mountain. Afternoon shade inland and desert or full sun in winter.

SEASON: Cool. Winter crop in the desert.

PLANTING METHOD: Seed.

CULTIVATION: For hot climates, start in containers well in advance for spring-planted crops harvested into

Curly kale becomes sweeter after a frost.

Collard greens are a staple of the South and are being discovered elsewhere due to their wide adaptability and nutritional value.

early summer. Sow at the end of summer for winter-harvested crops for longer yields. Later fall sowing is recommended for the desert.

FROST TOLERANCE: Yes. Tolerates cold to 5 degrees F; cold actually improves sweetness and flavor.

PESTS: Wooly aphids.

DISEASES: Few.

Broccoli and Cauliflower

TYPE: Biennial grown as annual crop. Cauliflower is more sensitive to heat and drought than broccoli, so for low-water gardens it's best kept in coastal areas to exploit the maritime climate.

Purple cauliflower adds color to your garden and in the kitchen.

The leaves as well as broccoli flower heads are edible, making this a doubly valuable crop.

VARIATIONS: Closely related, there are three similar variations: broccoli has green flower heads, cauliflower produces white, and the Romanesco is considered a cross between the two.

TRELLIS: No.

EXPOSURE: Full sun, coastal and mountain. Afternoon shade, inland and desert, or full sun in winter.

SEASON: Cool. Winter crop in the desert.

PLANTING METHOD: Seed.

CULTIVATION: For hot climates, start in containers well in advance of last frost so once planted out, plants have time to fully mature a main flower head, then, after it's cut, remain healthy enough to produce additional smaller side heads before high heat and dry conditions arrive.

FROST TOLERANCE: Yes.

PESTS: Worms, maggots.

DISEASES: Minimal.

Brussels Sprouts

TYPE: Biennial grown as annual crop.

TRELLIS: No, but staking may be required.

EXPOSURE: Full sun, coastal and mountain. Inland and desert, winter crop with afternoon shade.

SEASON: Cool. Winter crop in the desert, but may prove intolerant of low humidity levels.

PLANTING METHOD: Seed.

CULTIVATION: Best planted in fall for winter crop, where maritime coastal influence allows long yield.

Brussels sprouts are a great crop for winter in the high desert or mountain regions due to their tolerance of cold.

FROST TOLERANCE: Good.

PESTS: Worms, maggots.

DISEASES: Minimal.

Kohlrabi

TYPE: Biennial grown as annual crop.

TRELLIS: No.

ROW COVERS: Yes.

EXPOSURE: Full sun, coastal and mountain. Inland and desert, winter crop with afternoon shade.

SEASON: Cool. Winter crop in the desert.

PLANTING METHOD: Seed.

CULTIVATION: Plant in early spring for early crop, then again in fall for winter crop.

FROST TOLERANCE: Good.

PESTS: Worms, maggots.

DISEASES: Minimal.

Legume Tribe (Fabaceae Family)

This unique tribe thrives where other plants fail due to an ability to harvest atmospheric nitrogen rather than being dependent on that nutrient existing in soil.

The legumes are one of the most productive crops in dry and desert gardens, particularly since many strains of beans were developed in the Southwest. It's important to know that there are two types of beans: those with edible pods and those designed for dry storage.

Beans in general are warm-season crops. Dry beans were developed in the Southwest as part of the "Three Sisters" growing method that combines beans, corn, and squash together in the same spot. These will be the most heat and drought resistant. Green beans such as Kentucky Wonder are not as well adapted to low water levels and can suffer significantly if not sufficiently irrigated. Problems arise with pods becoming too fibrous due to lack of moisture.

Peas are a cool-season crop, which explains why its traditional planting date is March 17, significantly earlier than most other crops. Whether they're shelling peas, or edible-podded snow or snap peas, these plants are the children of the spring and don't fare well in the heat. Edible-podded peas also will suffer if not provided enough water. Water is often wasted when gardeners try to drive them to produce in a summer garden. In the low desert and very mild winter zones, planting can occur as early as January, so harvest is still in the cool season period.

Beans remain a vital nutritional source whether eaten green in the pod or dried.

Pole beans require a sizable trellis to support their very fast growth.

Bean

TYPE: Annual vine, with some bush types.

VARIATIONS: Bush or pole. Dry beans are grown to maturity and allowed to dry for harvest and long-term storage Snap beans are eaten with the pod at the young, tender, green stage.

TRELLIS: Pole bean is a twining vine that can climb on a net or wire trellis, or the time-tested pole teepee method.

EXPOSURE: Full sun.

SEASON: Warm.

Bush beans are more versatile forms that suit smaller gardens, greenhouses, and row covers.

PLANTING METHOD: Sow in ground after frost has passed. For containers, sow directly into potting soil.

CULTIVATION: Install trellis before sowing beans.

FROST TOLERANCE: None.

PESTS: Whiteflies, spider mites, cucumber beetles, aphids.

DISEASES: Minimal.

Peas

Dwarf snow peas allow this delicious Asian vegetable to be grown within row covers.

Peas require an upright trellis, such as a net or piece of woven wire fence.

TYPE: Annual vine.

VARIATIONS: Three types: shelling, edible-podded snap, and edible-podded snow. Snow peas fare better in low humidity and desert conditions, whereas snap peas easily become fibrous.

TRELLIS: Yes, with fine mesh. Dwarf forms won't need a trellis.

EXPOSURE: Full sun.

SEASON: Early cool season.

PLANTING METHOD: Sow in-ground, as soon as the ground can be worked.

CULTIVATION: In the low desert, sow in December, in warmer climates in February, and in temperate zones, St. Patrick's Day (March 17) is the traditional planting date.

FROST TOLERANCE: Yes.

PESTS: Aphids, cucumber beetles.

DISEASES: Powdery mildew, viruses, wilts.

Squash Tribe (Curcurbita Family)

This tribe requires a lot of room for large sprawling plants that cover much ground, but the yields are truly extraordinary.

This is an international group of vegetables that blends three continents to deliver our most productive crops. North America contributed squash from our own Native American strains. Africa is home to sweet melons that came to the hot American states of the south and west. Cucumbers traveled well beyond their Asian homeland to America, where they are grown for pickling, our time-tested home canning choice.

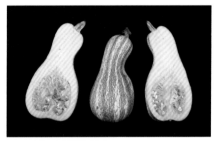

The squash variety, Navajo Trail, is an heirloom of Pueblo tribal agriculture.

What distinguishes this group of plants is their amazing habit of spreading far in long vine runners. They've reached a pinnacle with giant pumpkins, a distinctly American tradition. All squash are grown in the summer, but only the hard winter squashes such as butternut are cultivated for root-cellar storage. Because a single plant grows so large, these are ideal for drip irrigation applied directly to the base of the main stem versus other crops, such as corn, that require many individual emitters for more widespread delivery.

Cucumber

TYPE: Annual vine, with some bush types.

VARIATIONS: Long, smooth slicing types, short pickling types, and mild oddballs. Armenian cucumbers are, in fact, melons, but they grow and taste like cucumbers,

Lemon cucumbers are an old heirloom variety with a bright taste.

Cucumbers flower and fruit rapidly before extreme heat slows them down.

so they're in this section too. Burpless cucumbers have edible skin.

TRELLIS: Yes, although cucumbers can sprawl too, so they'll need lots of ground space.

EXPOSURE: Full sun.

SEASON: Warm.

PLANTING METHOD: Cucumbers like warm weather to germinate, then prefer cooler temperatures to mature, so starting plants ahead is the best solution. Sow into warm soil up to 2 weeks after the last frost in milder climates, or grow ahead in pots for an early spring crop in the desert.

CULTIVATION: Grow in elevated mounds with drip irrigation to prevent mildew.

FROST TOLERANCE: None.

PESTS: Cucumber beetles, flea beetles, aphids, whiteflies.

DISEASES: Mildew.

Squash

Squash blossoms shown here are bundled for sale in a Mexican market.

TYPE: Annual.

VARIATIONS: Summer squash is harvested immature when soft and sweet. Examples: yellow crookneck and zucchini. Winter squash is allowed to mature with a hard outer rind and is so named for its value as a winter storage crop. Examples: butternut and acorn.

TRELLIS: No.

EXPOSURE: Full sun.

SEASON: Warm.

PLANTING METHOD: Sow directly into warm soil.

CULTIVATION: Summer squash is more bush type. Winter squash produces long runner vines that demand a lot of space.

FROST TOLERANCE: None.

PESTS: Squash bugs, squash vine borers.

DISEASES: Minimal.

TIP: The broad leaves of summer squash have too much surface area to be exposed to high UV levels in the desert. The vast surface area is also prone to rapid moisture loss in the wind. In the desert, start them indoors well in advance for early spring planting after frost, or start ahead to plant in September for a much later crop.

Melons

TYPE: Annual vine.

VARIATIONS: Muskmelons and the cantaloupe group are ribbed fruits. Late melons include a variety of melons such as honeydew and casaba. Watermelon is a different type, not as closely linked as muskmelons are to late melons.

TRELLIS: Though these are vines, they are grown on the ground and require a lot of space. Smaller melons can be grown on a trellis, but the weight of the fruit requires individual cloth slings for support.

EXPOSURE: Full sun.

Mayo watermelon is a time-tested desert melon that takes heat in stride.

SEASON: Warm. Melons are a long-term crop requiring up to 4 months to mature in evenly hot conditions to develop full sweetness. They are not suited to shorter-season climates but can do very well in the desert.

PLANTING METHOD: Start ahead in containers or sow into warm soil.

CULTIVATION: Sow 2 weeks after the last frost date. Select more compact melon varieties to grow in smart boxes and large pots, but vines will still ramble far and wide.

FROST TOLERANCE: None.

PESTS: Aphids, cucumber beetle, mites, squash vine borers.

DISEASES: Fusarium wilt, powdery mildew.

Leafy Tribe (Brassica Family, Amaranth Family)

Greens are a most diverse tribe defined not by their genetics but by the edible part, the leaf, which can be eaten fresh, stir-fried, or stewed.

This group, which draws species from around the world, is divided into fresh greens and pot greens, which are cooked. Many pot greens, such as collards, are also from the Brassica Tribe. Swiss chard is surprisingly drought- and heat-resistant for spring and fall gardens. Asian greens alone are so numerous, they are a whole group unto themselves, with another Brassica, bok choy, proving highly adapted to hot, dry gardens. From Italy come arugula, another green that thrives in dry conditions. The lettuces, however, can be a challenge because they are prone to bolt and flower, the foliage becoming bitter with drought or heat. These are best adapted to the immediate Pacific Coast, while elsewhere they are best grown during winter in a greenhouse or beneath row covers where conditions are naturally moist and cool.

Lettuce

TYPE: Annual that bolts to flower with heat. Eaten fresh.

VARIATIONS: Crisphead is the most particular about heat and must be carefully timed. Loose leaf proves more amenable to heat with countless varieties. Butterhead is a smaller, thicker leaf lettuce. Romaine originates in the eastern Mediterranean and is more sturdy and upright, and adaptable to drier conditions.

TRELLIS: No.

EXPOSURE: Full sun, filtered shade in high-UV desert and mountain areas.

SEASON: Cool. Prefers greenhouse or maritime climate for best results.

PLANTING METHOD: Sow in ground or start ahead to plant out early. Lettuce will thrive in that short period after frost but before heat begins, so starting ahead brings more mature plants outside to exploit this narrow window.

CULTIVATION: Great choice for containers. Row covers are helpful to protect plants in low-humidity areas. Ideal greenhouse crop.

FROST TOLERANCE: None.

PESTS: Snails, slugs, worms, leaf miners, aphids.

DISEASES: Downy mildew, fusarium wilt.

TIP: Lettuce needs consistent moisture levels to prevent bitterness.

A huge range of tender salad greens can be grown from seed or seedlings purchased at a garden center.

Lettuce seed blended with an assortment of varieties and exotic greens make a perfect salad garden for small spaces and in row covers.

Swiss Chard

TYPE: Biennial grown as annual.

VARIATIONS: Red- or white-colored stewing greens.

TRELLIS: No.

EXPOSURE: Full sun, part shade.

Swiss chard is the easiest and fastest pot greens for the cool season garden though they can withstand considerable heat if protected from winds that tatter leaves.

SEASON: Cool.

PLANTING METHOD: Sow in ground or grow in containers. Red chard is popular for growing with flowering annuals on porch or patio.

CULTIVATION: Sow in late winter or early fall for cool-season greens that last all winter in milder zones.

FROST TOLERANCE: Marginal.

PESTS: Snails, slugs, aphids, cabbage worms, flea beetles, leaf miners.

DISEASES: Minimal.

Pseudo Spinach

TYPE: Due to the tendency of true spinach to bolt and go to seed quickly, spinach substitutes are common in warmer climates. New Zealand spinach is an evergreen perennial; Malabar spinach is a perennial vine.

VARIATIONS: NZ spinach is a groundcover that is dense and long-yielding with a valuable tolerance for salt and alkaline soil. Malabar is a vine from India renowned for its heat tolerance and larger, thicker leaves.

TRELLIS: Yes for Malabar.

EXPOSURE: Full sun.

SEASON: Warm.

PLANTING METHOD: As perennials, these can be planted once and produce for a very long time where frost is limited.

CULTIVATION: Sow after last frost into garden soil.

FROST TOLERANCE: None.

PESTS: Minimal.

DISEASES: Minimal.

Arugula, Endive, and Escarole

TYPE: Annual or biennial greens.

VARIATIONS: Broad leaf or curly leaf.

TRELLIS: No.

EXPOSURE: Full sun.

SEASON: Cool.

PLANTING METHOD: In ground. Ideally suited to pots on porch or patio.

CULTIVATION: Sow early in the year while conditions are mild, or sow in early fall for a later crop.

FROST TOLERANCE: None.

PESTS: Minimal.

DISEASES: Minimal.

Asian Greens

TYPE: Fast growing and maturing annuals and biennials.

VARIATIONS: Many specialty plants little known to western gardeners. Bok choy: many varieties. Mustard: broadleaf, Chinese leaves. Chinese broccoli: spicier and smaller.

TRELLIS: No.

EXPOSURE: Full sun in cool conditions, filtered sun in warmer locations. All are cool-season crops are best left out of the summer garden except at high elevations or on the coast.

SEASON: Cool.

PLANTING METHOD: Sow into soil or grow in containers.

CULTIVATION: Grow with ornamentals on porch or patio and in smart boxes.

FROST TOLERANCE: None.

PESTS: Cabbage worms, root maggots.

DISEASES: Minimal.

Root Tribe (Apiaceae Family, Amaryllidaceae Family)

Edible roots and tubers are amazing when fresh, but they also are winter fare from the root cellar.

Sometimes they offer a bonus of stewing greens. This group includes the fastest crop in the garden, radishes, which mature from seed in 28 to 35 days. Because the edible parts of these plants are roots, they depend on phosphorus more than nitrogen. Most can be planted in spring for fresh summer harvest of the root, then sown again in August for a late fall harvest, which often goes into the root cellar for winter storage. The most versatile of these are beets and turnips, which offer a bonus of fresh edible leaves during the growing season as well as the large, nutritious, bulbous root. Onions are planted from seed or "sets," which are little bulbs that speed up the time till harvest and provide edible green onion leaves during the growing season. These crops do well in the sandy soils of the desert, where the roots are free to grow down deep as with the carrot and wide for beets. Root crops can be a challenge to conform to drip irrigation, but if the ¼-inch tubing is spaced with inline emitters every 6 inches, each plant will grow to maximum size without crowding.

Radish

TYPE: Annual.

VARIATIONS: Round, long white, and daikon.

TRELLIS: No.

EXPOSURE: Full sun.

SEASON: Cool.

PLANTING METHOD: Sow into garden soil.

CULTIVATION: Plant in early spring and fall. Plant in intervals so this fast-to-mature crop can be harvested over a much longer season.

FROST TOLERANCE: None.

PESTS: Minimal.

DISEASES: Minimal.

Radishes sown in fall or spring are the fastest crop to mature providing zest to spring salads.

TIP: Daikon is a cool-season, slow-germinating Chinese radish with a huge root that is often planted to open up heavy clay soils for improved drainage.

Beet

TYPE: Biennial grown as annual.

VARIATIONS: Red or novelty-colored varieties.

TRELLIS: No.

EXPOSURE: Full sun.

SEASON: Cool. Bolts to flower and roots grow woody in the heat.

PLANTING METHOD: Sow into garden soil.

CULTIVATION: Plant in early spring and fall. Plant in intervals for harvest over a much longer season.

FROST TOLERANCE: None.

PESTS: Minimal.

DISEASES: Minimal.

Carrot

In addition to traditional carrots, many varieties feature unique festive colors.

TYPE: Biennial grown as annual.

VARIATIONS: Long market types for sandy ground. Half-long types for more dense soil. Dwarf carrots for containers. Purple, red, and white varieties available.

TRELLIS: No.

EXPOSURE: Full sun.

SEASON: Cool.

PLANTING METHOD: Sow into garden soil.

CULTIVATION: Plant in early spring and fall. Plant in intervals so crop can be harvested over a much longer season.

FROST TOLERANCE: No.

PESTS: Carrot rust flies, wire worms, nematodes.

DISEASES: Minimal.

Turnip, Rutabaga

TYPE: Biennial grown as annual.

VARIATIONS: Turnip varieties include globe and flattened globe, with various color patterns and edible foliage. Rutabaga is a much longer-term crop, up to 4 months, from seed to harvest.

TRELLIS: No.

EXPOSURE: Full sun. Summer turnips prefer some shade.

SEASON: Cool. Flavor of these root crops is altered if not adequately hydrated. Best sown early spring and fall.

PLANTING METHOD: Sow into garden soil.

CULTIVATION: Sow turnips in intervals of 2 weeks in spring to extend harvest.

FROST TOLERANCE: No.

PESTS: Armyworms, cabbage root maggot, flea beetles.

DISEASES: Minimal.

Onion and Garlic

TYPE: Biennial grown as annual.

VARIATIONS: Green onions grown from seed are scallions. Bulbing onions are mostly grown from sets (bulbs). Temperate zone onions are pungent, long-day varieties (needing 14 to 16 hours of sunlight). Intermediate-day onions suited to northern California and Nevada latitude need 12 to 14 hours of sun. Those for the desert and southern regions are short-day sweet varieties (10 to 12 hours). Onions must be suited to your latitude to produce properly. Garlic: Plant in early spring for summer harvest, or plant in fall.

TRELLIS: No.

EXPOSURE: Full sun.

SEASON: Cool.

PLANTING METHOD: Plant sets just under the soil so the very tip of the bulb is visible. Plant garlic cloves 2 inches deep.

It's easy to grow onions from small bulbs called sets, which are as easy to plant as a daffodil.

CULTIVATION: Plant sets and transplants 4 to 6 weeks before the last frost. Sow seed into garden when soil is at least 45 degrees F. Sow seed of short-day onions in the fall or early winter.

FROST TOLERANCE: None.

PESTS: Thrips, wireworms.

DISEASES: Mildew, which can be controlled with adequate air circulation.

Grains Tribe (Poaceae Family)

Corn

What makes corn challenging in dry climates is the way it is pollinated. Corn plants must be grown in groups and in close proximity so that pollen falling from the tassels on top can sift down to pollinate the ears located lower on the stalk. This demands a lot of space, and when using drip irrigation the lines must be carefully laid out to provide each plant with enough water, since corn can be a heavy feeder compared to other crops. Varieties developed in the desert Southwest by Pueblo tribes are less demanding of moisture, but most are for ground meal unless designated sweet corn.

Corn is best grown in blocks rather than rows to ensure complete pollination of each ear.

TYPE: Annual.

VARIATIONS: Sweet corn is eaten fresh. Popcorn, flint, flower, and dent are meal corn types. These varieties will cross-pollinate if grown close together, so keep sweet corn and popcorn separate for purity.

TRELLIS: No.

EXPOSURE: Full sun.

SEASON: Warm.

White kernel Hopi sweet corn is an excellent choice for desert gardeners.

PLANTING METHOD: Sow 2 weeks after last frost into warm soil. Plant in intervals if space permits to extend harvest.

CULTIVATION: Grow corn in blocks of shorter rows rather than a few long ones to ensure complete pollination. For Three Sisters tradition, or where block isn't feasible, create hills 3 feet in diameter with 6 to 8 seeds equally spaced, then thin to the three most vigorous plants per hill.

FROST TOLERANCE: None.

PESTS: Corn earworm.

DISEASES: Smut, a fungus caused by overly wet conditions.

Amaranth

Long before corn was developed in Mexico, the primary grain in the Americas was amaranth, a more civilized relative of pigweed. Seeds of this plant are renowned for their nutritional value as a rare complete protein. Small and black, they're used whole or ground into meal. This is a very drought-resistant grain that is excellent for desert gardens and produces well under drip irrigation in less-than-fertile soils. Early in the season the foliage of developing amaranth plants is an excellent pot green.

Amaranth grown by the Pima of the desert Southwest provided both nutritious leaves for pot greens and grains.

TYPE: Annual.

VARIATIONS: Highly variable colors of both flower heads and foliage with some short-stature plants suited to smaller spaces.

TRELLIS: No.

EXPOSURE: Full sun.

SEASON: Warm.

PLANTING METHOD: Sow into warm soil with slight covering over seed.

CULTIVATION: May be started ahead indoors to plant out after frost.

FROST TOLERANCE: None.

PESTS: Minimal.

DISEASES: Minimal.

MICRO GREENS, SPROUTING GREENS, AND OTHER SUPERFAST CROPS

NOTE: Many of these have a wide range of varieties best found in the Johnny's Selected Seeds catalog (see Resources).

- Arugula
- Chives
- Claytonia (Miner's lettuce)
- Cress
- Fenugreek
- Mustard
- Orach
- Purslane
- Radish
- Sorrel
- Spinach

Purslane is an edible succulent plant made famous by Thoreau who ate these "weeds" in Walden. *Note that many plants here often recognized as weeds are simply edible plants out of place.*

The term "seasonal" herbs applies to those that grow for a year or two, perhaps more depending on the severity of the winter. An annual herb such as basil grows from seed and matures in one season just like most vegetables, so these can be added to your rows. A biennial herb such as parsley has a two-year life cycle, growing from seed in year

Long-lived herbs can be harvested year-round from a greenhouse.

one, then returning in year two from roots that lie dormant over winter underground. This overwintering means you can't till the ground where biennial herbs grew in the first year, you harvest during the second year, and you must start over from seed in the third. There are some herbs that are technically more long-lived, such as parsley, or true perennials, which thrive for many years in milder winter zones, but are treated as annuals in colder winter regions.

COMMONLY GROWN HERBS

Sow basil in quantity for plenty of fresh cuttings and enough left over to dry for winter.

Basil

This popular culinary herb is an ideal summer plant to add to your vegetable garden. There are both green- and purple-foliage varieties as well as many other basil types from around the world that impart a range of flavors. This is the herb favored for pasta dishes and pesto. In the heat of summer, keep the flowers promptly clipped off the plants to extend your harvest.

Cilantro

This herb, also the source of coriander seed, is grown for its fresh foliage as accent flavoring for salsa and many other Latin American dishes. It is more unusual because there are two types of foliage. When grown as a winter crop in the tropical desert and as a cool-season annual elsewhere, the leaves are produced in a dense clumping plant. Sow new seeds every couple of weeks to keep your garden full of tender young plants. When temperatures rise, the plant bolts to flower, with the leaves changing to a more needle-like shape.

Parsley

This biennial is very slow to germinate from seed, so it is most often purchased as a seedling. In colder winter regions, such as dry mountain areas, the roots won't winter over to the second year. Parsley is also sensitive to dry ground, so you may have more difficulty growing this herb under low water conditions than the more-adaptable basil and cilantro.

LESS-COMMON SEASONAL HERBS

- Borage
- Cervil
- Cress
- Dill
- German chamomile
- Nasturtium
- Summer Savory

When you understand the tribal affiliations of the vegetable crops, you'll have the tools to better manage your growing operations. It requires some homework to understand how each crop fits into the highly variable schedules of desert climates or extends the harvest to its maximum with minimal moisture. The key is to pay attention to the nuances of your micro-local seasonal conditions, then strive to reconcile those patterns with different vegetable varieties or tribes. The more familiar you are with them, the better success you'll find in matching specific varieties to your local climate, the season you are planning for, and the minimal water supply you provide.

CHAPTER 10

Essentials and Problem Solvers

Since the last big western drought in the 1970s, the organic gardening world has been evolving toward less-water-consumptive food cultivation. Today there are many unique products and accessories that can make your effort to grow with less water easier and more successful.

INDISPENSABLE ROW COVERS

When you create a tunnel-like greenhouse over your garden rows, you use a row cover. Row covers have so many benefits that once you start using them you'll wonder how you ever gardened without them. Here is how a row cover can solve many food-garden problems:

▪ It can protect plants from cold damage. Use it to start seedlings in the garden while nights are still frosty, or to help mature plants live outdoors through the winter for year-round vegetables.

▪ It can shelter plants from high-UV sun damage in the desert.

▪ It can help conserve water. When you water a plant under a row cover, moisture in the soil gradually evaporates into the air. When there's a row cover present, the rising moisture lingers to humidify the air immediately around the plants, mitigating effects of low-humidity conditions and evaporative water loss.

Row covers are the most affordable and versatile way to protect plants from pests, sun, and wind in the desert.

- It protects against dry wind. Young vegetables are susceptible to desiccation from dry winds, and sensitive older plants are too. A row cover eliminates the need to create a windbreak for the whole garden by providing temporary or permanent smaller scale applications.

- It seals off plants from insect pests. Organic gardeners who do not use pesticides use lightweight row covers to create a "screen porch" for their vegetable crops. They are particularly useful for preventing whiteflies, aphids, and spider mites, which are very difficult to control. This is one of the best preventative tools for pest management.

REMEMBER POLLINATORS

Row covers for insect control have one drawback: they control all insects. This denies pollinators access to your plants, which prevents pollination of crops that depend on flowering, such as peas or peppers. This is why row covers are often used early in the plant's life span for a pest-free start, then are removed when plants flower to allow for pollination. If they are to remain in place during flowering, roll up the sides and open the ends to allow pollinator entry.

Row covers and greenhouses must be left open to allow pollinators to enter and fertilize when flowers first appear.

To allow the row cover to be rolled up for bed access and venting, some gardeners sow a sleeve on the long edge of each row cover and slide a piece of PVC into it. This allows it to roll up easily, be tied into place for the day, then rolled back down again for frost protection. Another trick is to use strong, high-quality wooden clothespins to temporarily hold row covers out of the way when working inside or as clamps for excess fabric in windy weather.

TYPES OF ROW COVERS

If your row cover was big enough, it would become a tunnel greenhouse! That's why it's best to consider them portable and temporary greenhouses in your garden. A row cover is composed of hoops and a cover sheeting that is made in different ways to serve a variety of purposes. For example, sheeting designed strictly for pest control will be a fine mesh that allows 100 percent of the sun to penetrate with free air flow while preventing even the smallest bugs from penetrating. On the other hand, plastic row covers designed strictly for frost protection are heavy-gauge, solid sheeting with high insulation values.

A row cover is composed of two elements: hoops and cover sheeting. Here are some variations:

FLEXIBLE HOOPS: Pressed into the soil for anchorage on each side to span a row or a series of closely spaced rows.

PREFABRICATED METAL HOOPS: These hoops are sold specifically for row covers, preshaped for different-sized arches. Often two hoops are used together to sandwich the row cover between them for better support, which is helpful in high wind coastal or desert regions.

HOMEMADE PVC HOOPS: Save money by using ½-inch PVC to create your own hoops. This is a great way to create a small greenhouse too.

TUNNEL ROW COVER

The standard row cover is also spun polypropylene but it's stronger, lasts longer, and offers some frost protection. This type is more dense, filters a greater amount of UV light, and may be removed and stored for years if well cared for. The medium- and heavyweight row covers require hoops to support the fabric so it does not crush plants or their flowering tips.

FLOATING ROW COVER

The most lightweight row cover, it is made of insect netting or spun-bonded polypropylene or polyester. It is so lightweight that it lays right on top of plants, rising as they grow, until the plants are mature enough to be exposed for pollination. This cover is also used on arching supports of wire mesh or PVC arches. These row covers have a shorter life span, sometimes lasting just one growing season.

TIP: Excellent row cover installation videos and articles, as well as professional assistance, are available at groworganic.com.

These wire panels are curved along the long side to create as much head space as possible for taller plants such as peppers.

TIP: The advantage to using woven row cover is that it's easy to repair if it's damaged or ripped. Keep dental floss and a mattress needle on hand to patch holes or close rips in a timely fashion before crops or the rest of the fabric is damaged.

SINGLE HOOP WITH SNAP CLAMPS: You can buy plastic Snap Clamps that snap around your PVC hoop to hold the cover tightly. These and other sheeting attachment fittings are sold in the row cover supply sections of most gardening catalogs. Clamps are a wise choice for windy regions where row covers are easily blown out of place.

COVER SHEETING: Row covers are typically composed of spunbonded polypropylene that's resistant to tearing and manufactured with different characteristics. Each one will be rated by its frost protection, light transmission, and weight. For example: Agribon AG-19 Floating Row Cover protects to 28 degrees F, allows 85 percent light transmission and weighs .55 oz. per square yard. Row covers by Agribon and other manufacturers can offer many different light and frost protection ratings within each of these five basic definitions.

ROW COVER FABRICS

TYPE	WEIGHT	HOOPS	FROST	LIFE SPAN
Insect Control	Lightest	No	No	Short
Floating Row Cover	Light	No	No	Short
Row Cover	Standard	Yes	Variable	Medium
Greenhouse Poly	Clear	Yes	No	Medium
Woven Poly	Heavy	Yes	Yes	Long

Floating Row Cover Installation (No Hoops)

SUPPLIES: Row cover fabric, staples.

1. Plant your bed in advance with seedlings or seeds.

2. Select a calm day for row-cover installation.

3. Unfold the row cover adjacent to the bed.

4. Cut to fit the bed's length.

5. Drape over the bed loosely.

6. Secure to the ground every 6 to 8 feet using staples, nails, or rocks, or use an anchor trench. Leave plenty of slack to allow for growth.

Very young seedlings are protected by a floating row cover laid upon wire mesh bent along the short side.

Tunnel Row Cover Installation (with PVC Hoops)

SUPPLIES: Row cover, hoops or PVC, rebar, garden staples, clamps.

1. Pound two pieces of rebar into opposite sides of the bed at a slight angle toward the center. Leave 6 inches exposed.

2. Slide PVC down over each rebar to create a hoop.

3. Repeat steps 1 and 2 for every 5 linear feet of tunnel.

4. Cut a piece of row cover measuring 8 feet longer than the length of the bed.

This tunnel row cover was designed for maximum wind resistance by using arched panels of welded wire mesh, which provide a flexible yet strong structure.

5. Lay out the row cover, allowing 4 feet extra on each end.

6. Clamp row cover snugly to both sides of each hoop.

7. Bury the edges of the row cover along both long sides of the tunnel, or stake into place.

8. Gather the loose end material and tie it with a cord.

9. Pound a stake into the ground and securely tie the cord to this anchor.

ROW COVER SUPPLY LIST (PER 5 LINEAR FEET OF TUNNEL)

- Two 18-inch pieces of ½-inch rebar (find in the masonry department of a home improvement store)
- Lengths of ¾-inch PVC pipe, 7 feet long (plumbing department)
- Supply of ¾-inch row cover clamps, two to four per pipe (order online)
- Row cover long enough for overall length of bed (order online)

While glass greenhouses may look great, they are very expensive and offer little space for large vegetable crops.

GREENHOUSES

In Israel, where desert food production is cutting edge, large tunnel greenhouses are indispensable for minimizing water demand and mitigating arid climatic conditions. In Southern California and Arizona, large-scale agricultural endeavors are growing peppers and other crops through the winter months within vast, warehouse-sized greenhouses. Both of these examples prove how well a greenhouse can solve problems and create opportunities in home gardens where water conservation is essential. This is also one of the best solutions for growing in the windy high desert, where low humidity and colder winters limit the growing season to short windows of time throughout the year.

When buying a greenhouse, be aware that there are DIY and hobby greenhouses, and more serious agricultural greenhouses for the dedicated grower. All are useful for growing plants with less water, but each have different design characteristics.

> **TIP:** The downside to greenhouses in very hot climates is the cumulative heat buildup during the summer months. When selecting a greenhouse for these areas, choose one with adequate ventilation higher up where heat collects. Hoop-style greenhouses with a rolled sheet covering can feature roll-up sides that release heat and allow seasonal cross-ventilation. In the desert, order a shade cloth cover for your greenhouse to reduce UV exposure during the sizzling summer months.

DIY Greenhouses

For those on a budget, the traditional DIY greenhouse is made with a pair of heavy beams set parallel, then spanned by arches of PVC covered with plastic or any of the materials utilized for row covers. The Internet offers many detailed plans for creating these enclosures for a fraction of the cost of a kit, but they may not be as strong in weather extremes.

Hobby Greenhouses

This type of greenhouse is available in a wide range of prices, depending on quality. On the low end are simple, wood-frame, peaked-roof units with a poly sheeting cover. On the high end are all-metal structures with glass panes. Whatever type you choose, always be conscious of what kind of strain is created by your local climate. Hobby greenhouses are notorious for succumbing to wind damage as they age, so in high-wind desert zones, seek ones with greater structural integrity.

Growers use large tunnel-shaped greenhouses. Each brand will produce shade covers specifically made to fit each of their models.

Benefits of hobby greenhouses:

- Affordable

- Fit easily into a small backyard

- Composed of a rigid structure

- Peaked-roof types are visually attractive

- High-end, glass-pane greenhouses are beautiful

- Suitable for small crops such as greens

- Excellent for starting crops ahead from seed

- May be used to overwinter plants in mild climates

- Easy to heat

Drawbacks:

- Less wind resistant than Quonset-style greenhouses

Agricultural Greenhouses

A Quonset-style greenhouse is used by professional growers of both ornamental and food crops. The high-tunnel design allows for evaporative cooling and ventilation to travel horizontally to efficiently keep temperatures low. Its dimensions are standardized in terms of height and width, but its length can be unlimited. A series of hoops set into a framework support different rolled coverings for adaptation to seasonal changes.

Benefits of agricultural greenhouses:

- Unlimited sizing based on grower needs

- Suitable for both poly sheeting and shade cloth

- Covers in-ground growing or raised beds

- Wide enough for bed depth and generous walkway

- Sides roll up during hot months

- Suited to evaporative cooling
- May be used to start seedlings early
- Easy DIY project
- More aerodynamic

Drawbacks:

- Not aesthetically appealing
- Difficult to heat due to greater interior area

This all-metal Quonset greenhouse produces amazing crops in a very windy part of the low desert.

Double-Walled Greenhouse Coverings

Double-walled greenhouse coverings are the best investment you can make. They offer far better insulation, resist tearing, and can be attached to the framework securely. A greenhouse made with double-walled coverings may allow you to grow food year-round without heating. When combined with passive-solar heating methods or designs, double-walled coverings can significantly expand your growing options.

In early spring, move overwintered tomato plants from the greenhouse outdoors, where fruit can ripen in the sun. Move pots to the garden, or plant them to allow for more expansive rooting.

However, double-walled coverings are sold in 4-foot-wide strips compared to the enormous sheeting used for traditional single-walled material. This makes them less versatile and more challenging to install or change. Here are two common types of double-walled materials:

SOLEXX: (Solexx.com) A flexible cover suitable for Quonset-style structures. This is a double walled material that is flexible but width is limited so it must be installed in many pieces much like wallpaper, which is more problematic than covering with a single sheet of standard greenhouse sheeting.

TWIN-WALLED POLYCARBONATE: A rigid product that proves an excellent alternative to single-walled corrugated fiberglass. If you have an existing fiberglass greenhouse, a peaked-roof wood frame, or any other type that doesn't have a curved roof, this option can be an excellent upgrade.

HYDRO STORES: A GOLDMINE

While the traditional local garden centers haven't changed much over the years, one supplier has cropped up in many towns: the hydroponic supply company. Chances are there's one near you, so check the yellow pages or go online. These shops can be your best resource for low-water-use gardening technology. The "hydro store" is usually an ordinary storefront, but inside you'll be amazed at the innovative products it contains. This is one of the best resources for seed-starting materials and indoor lights to help you get a head start on the season by exploiting late-winter rains. They're keen on timers and fertilizer injection systems for drip irrigation too. There's no end to what you'll find for solving problems, and you'll find wonderful products like pure kelp fertilizers too.

TRELLISES

A trellis is required for most climbing vegetable plants and others that need support when the weight of a heavy crop is too much. Failing to trellis properly can result in damage to stems and roots, where wounds can cause internal moisture loss or allow pests and diseases to enter the plant's vascular system. Failing to trellis can also cause plants to fall over, ripping apart the roots or tearing them out of the ground. This can result in inefficient utilization of soil moisture. Many trellis designs are simple DIY projects using wood and string or recycled materials. If you're not handy or the garden is in a high-profile area that must look good, consider investing in prefabricated metal trellises you'll use year after year. These are available online through Gardener's Supply Company, where you'll find the widest range of choices.

Some types of trellises:

- Vertical grid
- A-frame
- Cucumber
- Tunnel
- Tomato tower

A variety of different trellis structures are used on tomato plants. The small "tomato towers" sold everywhere are inadequate for big vigorous plants.

This simple 2-by-4-foot A-frame trellis with horizontal bamboo rods provides a strong structure to keep squash and melons off the ground.

Long poles set in the teepee style are ideal for pole beans that twine their way up the supports.

This simple bamboo pole trellis is lashed together with rope and vines climb up twine strung from top to bottom.

Climate modification accessories are key to water-conservative food gardening. When you grow in a greenhouse environment, there is minimal evaporation of the moisture you apply. In return, you enjoy unusual crops and a year-round organic harvest. For the scientifically minded, hydroponic food production is doable thanks to the hydro stores and their unique product lines. Though investing in these accessories will cost you more in the beginning, they will pay for themselves over time because you are not limited to the traditional growing season. While everyone else's garden is dormant, you may still have naturally ripened heirloom tomatoes for that fresh-cut salad of spring greens in January.

Resources

EASY START-UP CHECKLIST

Adjust the task months for your climate (see Chapter 1), but maintain the same order of tasks, as one builds upon the next.

AVERAGE MONTH	TASK	SHOP/ BUY	IN GARDEN	COMMENTS
November	Order seed catalogs			See page 192
November	Design garden			Crop rotation
December to January	Order seeds	X		Online
January	Pots and seed media	X		Local
February	Start seed indoors			Home
January to March	Order row covers	X		Online
March	Round up amendments	X	X	Local
March	Sketch drip diagram			Home
March to April	Plumb for drip system		X	Local
April	Purchase drip system	X		Local
April	Prepare soil		X	
May	Set up drip supply lines		X	
May	Plant seedlings		X	
May	Sow seed		X	
May	Set up row covers		X	
June to July	Mulch			

SUSTAINABILITY BEGINS AT HOME

Before you go online to buy gardening supplies, find out whether you can obtain what you need from local garden centers or hydroponic stores, because your purchases help support the gardening community in your area. This boosts small business and keeps your dollars in town, so you are helping grow greater consciousness of organic gardening and water conservation, and expanding the collective knowledge of what it takes to grow food during drought. This is a huge benefit to first-time gardeners.

   If your local retailer doesn't carry what you need but will order it, go that route. Your special order may begin long-term availability of those items in town for other gardeners to purchase. If you need it, chances are others will too.

ACCESS THE WORLD ONLINE

If shopping local doesn't completely satisfy your needs, the online world awaits. Online companies offer you the greatest range of products. Sometimes it's best to stay with time-tested, well-established resources because many smaller start-ups won't last long, leaving you to search once again for a more reliable source. However, with the explosion of interest in heirloom seeds and organic gardening problem solvers related to drought, some newer companies have proven themselves.

SEEDS AND PLANTS

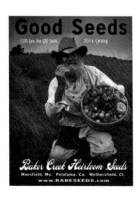

- Baker Creek Heirloom Seed Co.; 2278 Baker Creek Rd., Mansfield, MO 65704; (417) 924-8917; RareSeeds.com
- W. Altee Burpee & Co.; 300 Park Ave., Warminster, PA 18974; (800) 333-5808; Burpee.com
- Fedco Seeds; PO Box 520, Waterville, ME 04903; (207) 426-9990; FedcoSeeds.com
- High Mowing Organic Seeds; 76 Quarry Rd., Wolcott, VT 05680; (802) 472-6174; HighMowingSeeds.com

- Johnny's Selected Seeds; 955 Benton Ave., Winslow, ME 04901; (877) 564-6697; JohnnySeeds.com

- John Scheepers Kitchen Garden Seeds; PO Box 638, Bantam, CA 06750; (860) 567-6086; KitchenGardenSeeds.com

- Native Seed/SEARCH; 3584 E. River Road, Tucson, AZ 85718; (866) 622-5561; NativeSeeds.org

- Nichols Garden Nursery; 1190 Old Salem Rd. NE, Albany, OR 97321; (800) 880-7228; NicholsGardenNursery.com

- Renee's Garden; 6060 Graham Hills Rd., Felton, CA 95018; (888) 880-7228; ReneesGarden.com

- Seed Savers Exchange; 3094 W Winn Rd., Decorah, IA 52101; (563) 762-7333; SeedSavers.org

- Seeds of Change; PO Box 152, Spicer, MN 56288; (888) 762-7333; SeedsOfChange.com

- Southern Exposure Seed Exchange; PO Box 460, Mineral, VA 23117; (540) 894-9480; SouthernExposure.com

- Territorial Seed Company; PO Box 158, Cottage Grove, OR 97424; (800) 626-0866; TerritorialSeed.com

- The Cook's Garden; PO Box C5030, Warminster, PA 18974; (800) 457-9703; CooksGarden.com

Products and Supplies

To take advantage of all the products and supplies you'll need to grow food in a water-efficient way, the best resources are tried-and-true retailers that specialize in the things you'll need. These businesses, catalogs, and their online counterparts are also rich in information, and the sales staff are authorities who can help you purchase exactly what you need to protect plants, extend the season, limit water usage, and grow organically.

Two companies produce the quasi-hydroponic self-watering containers detailed in Chapter 3: EarthBOX (EarthBOX.com) and Grow Box (AGardenPatch.com).

The four online retailers listed below are the top companies in each area of interest. Each offers a full-color catalog and online shopping. It's wise to utilize all of them if you're serious about growing organic food with limited water. Each one will offer a distinctly different approach, while some things will overlap with all of them. Knowing where to get what you need quickly and efficiently helps you save money and assures you get exactly what's required when it's not available at local retailers. In the process of perusing these catalogs, you'll learn a great deal and discover a wide range of products you never knew existed. This is where you'll find high- and low-tech solutions for your unique challenges of climate, soils, and dwindling water availability.

General Gardening: Gardeners Supply Company (Gardeners.com)

This retailer has been around a long time and features a useful array of products you may not find locally. This is the place to buy stackable corners to build raised beds with locally sourced lumber. For rank beginners, this is the place to begin, using their in-house lines of no-brainer irrigation and growing supplies.

- Raised-bed kits
- Metal stackable corners for assembling raised beds
- Unique and functional trellis options
- Deer fencing
- Seed-starting kits and lighting
- Rain barrels and systems

Organic Farming: Peaceful Valley Farm Supply (GrowOrganic.com)

Peaceful Valley has been around for decades and has earned its place as the best resource for organic farmers who sell at your local farmers markets. Because these farmers must be certified organic, you know that virtually everything in this catalog is safe and effective. This retailer offers some of the most valuable blended fertilizers in bulk quantities, compared to the small bags or boxes you'll find locally.

- Large quantity seed-starting containers and systems
- Broad range of mycorrhizae and other inoculant microbes
- Floating row covers and shades
- Greenhouse and cold frame kits
- Liquid organic fertilizers for drip system injector systems
- A mind-boggling array of unusual organic fertilizers
- Beneficial insects
- Highly specific organic pest control products, traps, and deterrents
- Organic seed onions, potatoes, and garlic, plus vegetable seed

Drip Irrigation: DripWorks (DripWorks.com)

While you'll find drip-irrigation fittings and tubing at garden centers, local retailers rarely have the kind of specialized products you'll need to create an efficient, carefree system to water your garden. DripWorks is the most extensive catalog, geared for average gardeners as well as professionals. They are an excellent resource for drip system kits to get you started, and their more extensive listings for unique additions to the kit will ensure everything goes together perfectly.

- Drip system starter kits
- Timers: electronic, battery operated, solar
- Soaker dripline with variable spacing of preinstalled emitters
- Wide range of emitter types and sprinklers
- Drip tape kits for row crops

- Assorted fittings and accessories

- Fertilizer injectors for drip systems

Agriculture: FarmTek (FarmTek.com)

 This general-purpose agricultural catalog is one of the most useful resources for home gardeners and homesteaders. This is a dream book of everything imaginable that would be useful on today's modern farm or ranch. This is where commercial growers, nurseries, and large-scale hydroponic operators buy everything from enormous buildings to tiny drip emitters. This is the best place to obtain large sections of shade cloth and geotextiles. Catalogs are sent out numerous times over the year, coordinated for seasonal needs. While newbies may find it a bit overwhelming, seasoned gardeners will be thrilled to find so many problem solvers they never knew existed.

- Shade cloth, in many different densities and large sizes

- Deer and livestock fencing

- Netting, woven and molded

- Weed barrier fabric and geotextiles, in large sizes

- Rodent and pest-control barriers

- Hoop houses, high tunnels, and greenhouses

- Greenhouse heating and cooling systems

- Soil warmers and bottom heat

- Carts and wagons

- Buildings and fabric structures

Live Beneficial Insects

- Arbico-Organics.com
- Buglogical.com (an Arizona company familiar with desert conditions)
- PlanetNatural.com

REFERENCE BOOKS

Brookbank, George. *Desert Gardening: The Complete Guide*. Tucson, AZ: Fisher Books, 1991.

Deardorf, David, and Kathryn Wadsworth. *What's Wrong With My Vegetable Garden? 100% Organic Solutions for All Your Vegetables from Artichokes to Zucchini*. Portland, OR: Timber Press, 2011.

Kourik, Robert. *Drip Irrigation for Every Landscape and All Climates*. White River Junction, VT: Chelsea Green, 2009.

Lancaster, Brad. *Rainwater Harvesting for Drylands and Beyond*. White River Junction, VT: Chelsea Green, 2006.

Lowenfels, Jeff, and Wayne Lewis. *Teaming With Microbes: The Organic Gardener's Guide to the Soil Food Web*. Portland, OR: Timber Press, 2010.

Lowenfels, Jeff. *Teaming With Nutrients: The Organic Gardener's Guide to Optimizing Plant Nutrition*. Portland, OR: Timber Press, 2013.

Ludwig, Art. *Create an Oasis With Greywater: Choosing, Building and Using Greywater Systems*. Santa Barbara, CA: Oasis Design, 1991, Rainharvest.com.

Nabhan, Gary Paul. *Growing Food in a Hotter, Drier Land: Lessons from Desert Farmers on Adapting to Climate Uncertainty*. White River Junction, VT: Chelsea Green, 2013.

Shein, Christopher. *The Vegetable Gardener's Guide to Permaculture*. Portland, OR: Timber Press, 2013.

Glossary

ANNUALS: The majority of vegetable crops are called "annuals," a term that is derived from the Latin root word *annus* or year. These plants complete their entire life cycle in the span of a single year or, more accurately, a single growing season. All are programmed to hurry up and produce seed before they die with frost in the fall, since this is the way their species survives. This drive to reproduce is a powerful force that lies within our annual vegetable crops.

COOL-SEASON CROPS: These vegetables germinate in cooler soils averaging about 40 degrees F or warmer, and prefer cooler temperatures to produce edible foliage. These crops bolt at 90 degrees F, but they also are stimulated by long day length. Examples: kale, lettuce, and chard.

DESERTIFICATION: The process of fertile land transforming into desert due to inappropriate agriculture, deforestation, drought, or a combination of factors.

DESICCATION: The drying out of a living organism, such as what happens to plants when they are exposed to sunlight or drought. To gardeners in dry times, it's the rate of desiccation that matters most. The larger a plant leaf surface, the more rapidly it desiccates. When conditions are extreme, the rate of desiccation can be so great the plant will not be able to draw up enough moisture from the roots to replace the amount lost. The result is temporary wilt. If temporary wilt continues long enough, permanent wilt kills the leaf, growing tip, or entire plant.

EPHEMERALS: The word "ephemeral" is defined as anything that lasts for a very short time. Compared to long-lived perennials, vegetable crops are true ephemerals that live during one growing season. Each kind of vegetable has a designated life span, which is typically shown on a seed packet. For example, one of the most ephemeral vegetables is the radish, which is ready to pick just three weeks after sowing if conditions are right.

EVAPOTRANSPIRATION (ET): The sum of soil moisture evaporation and plant transpiration from soil to the atmosphere.

FILTER: The small diameter of drip system fittings make them vulnerable to clogging. A filter is standard with your system to catch particulate matter in the water before it enters the smaller-diameter fittings. You won't have to clean the filter often with city water, but if your water source is a rain barrel or pond, or if you have hard, mineral-rich water, it may require more frequent cleaning to maintain peak efficiency.

FLOATING ROW COVER: The most lightweight row cover, it is made of insect netting or spun-bonded polypropylene or polyester. It is so lightweight that it lays right on top of plants, rising as they grow, until the plants are mature enough to be exposed for pollination. This cover is also used on arching supports of wire mesh or PVC arches. These row covers have a shorter life span, sometimes lasting just one growing season.

GPM/GPH: Irrigation heads used for lawns and flower beds have a rating in gallons per minute (GPM). A drip irrigation emitter delivers water so slowly that it's rated at gallons per hour (GPH).

GRAVITY FLOW: The effects of gravity on how rapidly water flows downhill and how much pressure can build up in the process.

HEAD PRESSURE: The amount of pressure, expressed in "feet of head," it takes to push the level of water higher in a standpipe. For example, gravity-fed water coming down-slope may force water up a vertical pipe.

HEAT ISLAND: An urban condition that keeps city spaces hotter than normal at night. It's caused by the amount of heat absorbed by paving, walls, and structures during the course of a summer day. This absorbed heat can be significant. In open rural areas, the heat that accumulates during the day rises after sunset to allow cooler air to take its place. In a city, where there can be little to no air movement, the heat in these thermal masses is released into the surrounding spaces, preventing them from cooling off.

HEIRLOOM: A term of affection for an old cultivar or landrace still in cultivation and thus available to buy from seed. The trend toward growing heirlooms helps keep varieties in continuous cultivation, which is the only way to preserve that plant's unique genetic characteristics for posterity.

HUMUS: A finely textured material, such as finished compost, resulting from organic matter consumed in the decomposition process. Humus can hold up to 80 percent of its weight in moisture.

HYBRID: The result of two species that cross-pollinate naturally or are crossbred artificially by plant breeders. The seed produced from this cross will carry some genetic characteristics of either parent, with highly variable results. Seed of hybrid plants can be sterile.

HYDROSTATIC PRESSURE: In plants, the condition of being fully hydrated, with cells and tissues filled to capacity with moisture. The term is akin to blood pressure in a human being. When a plant can't access adequate water, the tissues soften because the individual cells have lost moisture too. Loss of hydrostatic pressure leads to wilt and other problems.

LANDRACE: Vegetable varieties developed by farmers and gardeners around the world that are super-adapted to the local microclimate. If that farmer ceases to replant his landrace, it will vanish from existence when the last viable seed dies.

MACRONUTRIENTS: The three chief macronutrients in soil are nitrogen, phosphorus, and potassium. Nitrogen is responsible for stem and leaf growth and is vital to leaf crops. Phosphorus and potassium are linked to roots, flowers, and fruit production vital to most vegetable plants.

MICROBES: A wide range of microscopic organisms that live in soil, feed on organic matter, and offer a wide range of benefits to plants.

MICRONUTRIENTS: These nutrients are needed for plant growth but in much smaller amounts; sometimes just a trace is required. The most important are boron, chlorine, copper, iron, manganese, molybdenum, and zinc.

MICRO-SPRAY EMITTER: This emitter functions like a standard sprinkler head in low-pressure drip systems. It's set atop a pencil-like spike that moistens an area about 12 inches in diameter. Spray emitters won't wet the soil as deeply as standard emitters and may promote surface rooting.

MITIGATE: To make something less severe, serious, or painful. In the landscape, the process of problem solving is often called mitigation of undesirable conditions.

MYCORRHIZAE: Fungal organisms that actually enter the roots of plants to live symbiotically for the benefit of both. One type of mycorrhizae, often called the "inoculant," allows leguminous plants to utilize atmospheric nitrogen and transfer it into the soil.

OMRI LISTED: When you consider pest control products for your organic garden, many of them will state on the package that they're OMRI Listed. This means the Organic Materials Review Institute has evaluated this product and its contents to verify it is indeed an organic product. This independent review is necessary for a certified organic farmer to use it. While many products claim to be "organic," those that bear the OMRI seal are proven organic.

ORGANIC MATTER: A wide range of matter derived from plants and animals. When added to soil, microbes break it down into a simpler form utilized by living plants.

PSI: Pounds per square inch (PSI) is the way water pressure at the faucet is rated. A common rating for residential water supply is 60 PSI. A drip system operates at 15 to 30 PSI. Static PSI in your neighborhood can drop in the morning when everyone is in the shower, which can sometimes affect traditional sprinkler system performance.

SEED BANK: A place where seed with long-term viability can be preserved. Seed banks help to preserve genetic diversity that may prove the salvation of the food supply as climates change.

STRUCTURE: The relative percentages of sand, silt, and clay in your soil. Sand will be the most porous and easy to work, clay will be the densest. Soil structure is crucial to how the water you apply behaves within the soil and whether it drains properly.

SUPPLY LINE: The standard supply line for a drip system is made of ½-inch diameter flexible tubing that brings water quickly to smaller lateral lines that feed emitters. You can add "in line" emitters directly to the ½-inch supply line to deliver more water to row crops.

TRANSPIRATION: The process of water movement through a plant and its evaporation from aerial parts, such as from leaves, but also from stems and flowers.

TUNNEL ROW COVER: The standard row cover is also spun polypropylene but it stronger, lasts longer, and offers some frost protection. This type is more dense, filters a greater amount of UV light, and may be removed and stored for years if well cared for. The medium- and heavyweight row covers require hoops to support the fabric so it does not crush plants or their flowering tips.

VIABILITY: The length of time a seed remains "alive" to grow into a plant. A short-term viability example is certain lettuce that loses viability after just one year. The record for extended viability is date seed from ruins thousands of years old that successfully germinated.

WARM-SEASON CROPS: These vegetables germinate at soil temperatures from 60 to 75 degrees F, and depend on heat to flower and produce fruit. Examples: tomato, squash, and beans.

Acknowledgments

I could not have written this book without the help of my husband, Jim Gilmer, who has supported my efforts, listened patiently to my ideas, and assisted with photography for this book. Thank you to Jeanne Fredericks, my beloved literary agent who helped to shape this work and bring it to market. Much appreciation to Hannah Elnan, the enthusiastic far-sighted acquisitions editor who recognized the value of problem-solving books for drought. Finally, thank you everyone at Sasquatch Books for all the behind-the-scenes efforts from copyediting to special sales. Together we may all bring solutions to gardeners during this epic drought in the West.

Index

NOTE: Photographs are indicated by *italics*.

A

amaranth, 174–175, *174*
annuals, xii, 84, 198
ants, 99
aphids, 99, 105
arugula, 167
Asian greens, 125, 168
autumn equinox, *142*, 143

B

Bacillus thuringiensis. See Bt
basil, 176, *176*
beans, 124, 159–160, *159*
beets, 124, 170
biocontrols, 98–99, 105
birds, 100–101, *106*
Blass, Simcha, 76–77
broccoli, 124, 156–157, *156*
brussels sprouts, 157, *157*
Bt (*Bacillus thuringiensis*), 98–99, 100, *100*

C

cabbage, 124, 154–155, *155*
caliche, 50–51
carrots, 170–171, *170*
caterpillars, *99*, 100, *101*
cats, 96, *96*
cauliflower, 124, 156–157, *156*
cilantro, 176–177
cisterns, 89–90
climate modification, 23–40
climates, 3–21

growing seasons, 3–11, 144–147
  selecting vegetables, 114–115, *116–117*,
  123–125
cloches, 134–135, *134*
coastal regions, 9–10, *9*, *10*, 123–125
coir, 68
cold air drainage, 147–148
collards, *112*, 155–156, *156*
compost, 64, 66–67, *67*, 71, *71*
container gardening, 43–47, 48
cool-season crops, xiii, 84, 143, 144–147,
  198
corn, 125, 173–174, *173*
cucumbers, 124, 161–162, *162*

D

day length, 142, *142*
desertification, 23, 198
desert regions, xv, 50–51, 60, *60*
  high, 4–5, *4*, *5*, 123–125, 146–147
  low, 7, *7*, 123–125, 144–146
desiccation, 4, 198
drip irrigation, 75–86, 97, 135, 195–196
Dust Bowl, 32, *32*, 93

E

eggplants, 123, 152–153, *152*
emitters by crop, 81–82
endive, 167
ephemerals, xii–xiii, 198–199
escarole, 167
evapotranspiration (ET), 11–21, 199

F

fencing, 29–30, *30*, 102–103, *103*
  See also wind barriers
fertilizers. *See* soil
filters, 85, 199
fish emulsion, 65, *66*, *71*
floating row covers, 181, 182, 183, *183*,
  199

G

garden beds
  in-ground, 49, *54*, 55–57
  raised, 48–54
garden design, 23–25, *24*, *25*
garden location, 26–31
garden size, 56–57
garlic, 172
glossary, 198–202
GMOs (genetically modified organisms),
  113
GPM/GPH (gallons per minute/hour), 78,
  199
gravity flow, 87, 199
gray-water harvesting, 90–91
greenhouses, 39–40, *40*, 184–188
greens, 125, 164–168
growing seasons
  cold air drainage, 147–148
  cool- vs. warm-season crops, xiii–xiv, 84,
    143, 144–147
  local climates, 3–11, 144–147
  overview, 141–144
  seeds vs. seedlings, 129–130
  start-up checklist, 191

H

hard water, 79, *79*, *80*
head pressure, 88, 199
heat. *See* sun exposure; temperature

heat islands, 14, 19, 199–200
hedges, 36, *36*
heirlooms, 112, 120–122, 200
herbs, 176–177
hornworms, 100, *100*, 105
hoses, 77, 78, 86–87, *86*, *87*
humidity, 13, 16, 20
humus, 59, 200
hybrids, 118, 200
hydroponics, 44–46, 48, 63, 188
hydrostatic pressure, 5, 200

I

insects and pests, 93–106, 139
  beneficial, 94–96, *94*, *95*, 180, *180*, 197
  solutions for, 94, 96–99, 102–105
irrigation. *See* drip irrigation

K

kale, 124, 155–156, *155*
kelp, 65, 66
kohlrabi, 158

L

landraces, 111, 200
legumes, 158–161
lettuce, 125, 165, *165*

M

macronutrients, 65, 200
manures, 62, 66–67, 70
melons, 125, 163–164, *163*
microbes, 59, 63–64, 66, 85, 200
micro greens, 175, *175*
micronutrients, 65, 201
micro-spray emitters, 75, *76*, 201
mitigation, 24, 201
monsoon season, 6, *6*

mountains, 8, *8*, *9*, 123–125
mulch, 62–63, *62*, 69–71, *71*
mycorrhizae, 63–64, 66, 201

N

NOAA (National Oceanic and Atmospheric
   Administration), 21

O

ollas, 89
OMRI (Organic Materials Review
   Institute), 99, 201
onions, 172, *172*
organic matter, 61–63, 201

P

palm fronds, 35, *35*, 62–63, *62*
parsley, 177
peas, 124, 160–161, *160*
peat, 67
peppers, 123, 151–152, *151*, *152*
pesticides, 94–95, 98, 99, 105
planter mixes, 67, *68*
planting dates. *See* growing seasons
pollinators, 180, *180*
potatoes, 153–154, *153*
potted seedlings, 131–134, 138
potting soil, 47
probiotics, 64, 66
PSI (pounds per square inch), 78, 201

R

radishes, 169, *169*
rain, 6, *6*, 13–14, 17–18
rainwater harvesting, 55, 87–88, *88*
resources, 118–122, 191–198
rodents, 101–104, *102*, *103*, *104*
rooting medium, 134

rototillers, 54, 55–56, *56*
row covers, *96*, 97, 101, *101*, 179–184
rutabaga, 171

S

scale insects, 99
seasons. *See* growing seasons
seed banks, 113, 202
seeds and seedlings, 129–139
seed sources, 118–122, 192–193
self-watering containers (SWC), 44–46, *45*,
   46, 48
shade cloths, 37–39, *38*, *39*
shelterbelts, 37
soap, insecticidal, 98
soil, 14, 17–18, 59–72
   desert, 50–51, 60, *60*
   drainage, 18, 28, *29*, 61
   fertilizers and amendments, 61–62,
      64–69, 70, 71, *71*
   microbes, 59, 63–64, 85
   potting soil, 47
   seed starting media, 134, 138
   See also mulch
soil conditioners, 67
sowing seeds, 135
spinach, pseudo, 166–167
spring equinox, *142*, 143
sprouting greens, 175
squash, 123–124, 161, *161*, 162–163, *162*
structure, soil, 60, 202
summer solstice, 142, *142*, 143
sun exposure, 19, 27–28, 37–39
supply lines, 81, 202
Swiss chard, 125, 166, *166*

T

temperature, 13, 14, 16, 19–20, 21
terraces, 57
tomatillos, 151

tomatoes, xii–xiii, 130
   growing guide, 149–150, *149, 150*
   pests, 100, *101, 102*, 105
   varieties, 112, 123, 151
transpiration, 12, 202
trees, 30–31, *31*, 36–37
trellises, 188–189, *189*
tunnel row covers, 181, 182, 183–184, *184*, 202
turnips, 171

V

valleys, inland, 10–11, *10, 11*, 123–125
vegetables, selecting, 111–126
vegetables, types of, 148–177
vertical gardening, 48
viability, 114, 202

W

waffle gardens, 23–25, *24, 25*
warm-season crops, xiii–xiv, 84, 143, 144–147, 202
water and watering, 75–91
   conservation methods, 55, 86–91
   container gardening, 43–47
   evapotranspiration, 11–21, 199
   garden location, 27
   "leaky pipe," 78
   rodent tunnels and, 101–102
   seeds/seedlings, 133, 135, 137–138
   vertical gardening, 48
   See also drip irrigation; rain
water pressure, 78
weather reports, 21, 37
wind, 12–13, 15–16
wind barriers, 33–37
windrows, 36–37
winter solstice, 142, *142*, 144

Photograph by Maureen Gilmer

About the Author

MAUREEN GILMER is a syndicated garden columnist and author of eighteen books on gardening and landscaping design. She lives in Palm Springs, California, in the heart of the desert.

Find out more at **MoPlants.com**.